THE SIZE OF THE SLAVE POPULATION AT ATHENS DURING THE FIFTH AND FOURTH CENTURIES BEFORE CHRIST

BY

RACHEL LOUISA SARGENT
A.B., Bates College, 1914
A.M., University of Illinois, 1917

THESIS
SUBMITTED IN PARTIAL FULFILLMENT OF THE REQUIREMENTS FOR
THE DEGREE OF DOCTOR OF PHILOSOPHY IN CLASSICS IN THE
GRADUATE SCHOOL OF THE UNIVERSITY OF ILLINOIS, 1923

GREENWOOD PRESS, PUBLISHERS
WESTPORT, CONNECTICUT

Library of Congress Cataloging in Publication Data

Robinson, Rachel Sargent, 1891-
    The size of the slave population at Athens during
the fifth and fourth centuries before Christ.

    Reprint of the 1924 ed. of the author's thesis,
University of Illinois, 1923.
    Bibliography: p.
    1. Slavery in Greece. I. Title.
HT863.R6 1973   301.44'93'09385   73-10760
ISBN 0-8371-7034-6

301.44
R663s

Originally published in 1924 by the University of Illinois,
Urbana

Reprinted from an original copy in the collections of the
University of Illinois Library

Reprinted in 1973 by Greenwood Press, Inc.
51 Riverside Avenue, Westport, CT 06880

Library of Congress catalog card number 73-10760
ISBN 0-8371-7034-6
81-3700
Printed in the United States of America

10 9 8 7 6 5 4 3 2

TABLE OF CONTENTS

PREFACE

It is a pleasure to express here my thanks to Professor W. A. Oldfather at whose suggestion this investigation was begun, and through whose guidance and inspiration it has been completed. Furthermore, I am indebted to him for the privilege of consulting his unpublished bibliography on social and economic conditions in the ancient world. To Professor A. S. Pease of Amherst College, I am also under deep obligation for much valuable criticism of each chapter and many helpful suggestions. Both Dr. J. J. Parry of the English Department and Dr. W. A. Oldfather have given me able and generous assistance in the reading of the proof.

INTRODUCTION

Many questions pertaining to the social and economic life of the ancient Greeks cannot be satisfactorily answered until the relative numbers of the slave workers and the free have been more precisely determined. Realizing the importance of this problem, many scholars, since 1752, have treated the subject, some in a rather detailed, others in a more superficial fashion. The many discussions, as we shall see, have been centered about the very few passages left us which contain statistics about the slave population. But the numbers in these, unfortunately, are either ambiguously stated, and therefore subject to widely differing interpretations, or they are open to the charge of being untrustworthy, so that no general agreement has yet been reached as to the probable size of the slave population of ancient Greece. There is, however, a certain degree of unanimity. Most investigators of the problem now admit that for the slaves of Athens, Corinth, and Aegina the numbers 400,000, 460,000, and 470,000, respectively, occurring in the writings of one author only, of the second century after Christ, are absurdly high. They agree, also, that all free-born Greeks did not live lives of luxurious ease with their every wish gratified by service from a horde of slaves. It is, however, surprising to note that many persons who are led incidentally in their writings to allude to this phase of Greek life appear to attach little value to the results of these researches, for the figures 400,000 and more are still being cited as though these were authoritative and unquestioned estimates of the numbers of slaves. A few expressions on the part of authors of recent and widely read books may be quoted, merely to show the extent of this exaggeration of the importance of slavery in the city states of Greece, and especially Athens.

For example, Mr. G. Lowes Dickinson in *The Greek View of Life*[1] writes: "In the majority of the Greek states the slaves were the greater part of the population; in Athens, to take an extreme case, at the close of the fourth century they are estimated at 400,000 to the 100,000 citizens. . . . They existed simply to maintain the aristocracy of citizens, from whom and in whom the state had its being." A well-known text-book[2] by Haines and Haines

[1] (1913), 76.
[2] *Principles and Problems of Government* (1921), 15 f.

contains this remark: "The Greek democracies were little better than oligarchies, for about three-fourths of the population were slaves. The free citizens constituted the small leisure class who did no disagreeable work but devoted their time to government, fine arts, and refinements of life." Mr. H. M. Hyndman[3] uses more exaggerated language: "Numbers appeared to give the slaves no confidence. Such partial plots as were set on foot were rendered futile by treachery among the slaves themselves. . . . In Athens and Attica generally this is the more remarkable since not only were the slaves, as elsewhere, immensely preponderant in numbers to the extent of fourteen slaves to one adult citizen, but they also provided from their ranks the entire body of armed police." Very distorted is the picture lately drawn for young people in a book[4] in which there are entertainingly set forth as facts, statements questioned or refuted as much as a century and a half ago, and many times since then: "The Greek city, therefore, whenever it was not ruled by a king or tyrant, was run by and for the free men, and this would not have been possible without a large army of slaves who outnumbered the free citizens at the rate of six or five to one and who performed those tasks to which we modern people must devote most of our time and energy if we wish to provide for our families and pay the rent of our apartments. The slaves did all the cooking and baking and candle-stick making of the entire city. They were the tailors and the carpenters and the jewelers and the school teachers and the book-keepers and they tended the store and looked after the factory while the master went to the public meeting to discuss questions of war and peace, or visited the theatre to see the latest play of Aeschylus or hear a discussion of the revolutionary ideas of Euripides, who had dared to express certain doubts upon the omnipotence of the great god Zeus. Indeed, ancient Athens resembled a modern club. All free-born citizens were hereditary members and all the slaves were hereditary servants, and waited on the needs of their masters, and it was very pleasant to be a member of the organization. . . . The slaves took care of those tasks which now-adays are performed by business men and professional men."

[3] *Evolution of Revolution* (1920), 69.
[4] H. Van Loon, *The Story of Mankind* (1921), 66 ff.

In view of these generalizations[5] which are frequently being made to a large and, in the main, uncritical audience, it seems to be time to re-examine the data upon which our knowledge of the slave population in ancient Greece, and particularly in Attica, is based. Because, however, the results of the many researches made hitherto are so generally overlooked, there appears to be needed, first of all, a summary of the work of previous investigators. This will be attempted in the first chapter of this study, with a brief indication of what has been already accomplished and what there is left for others to add. In the succeeding chapters, it is proposed to present from the literature of the fifth and fourth centuries before Christ the evidence, direct or indirect, from which there could, with some assurance, be inferred how many slaves average persons in Athens (a term here used synonymously with Attica) of the wealthy, middle, or poor classes actually owned and for what purposes. In the passages cited as evidence, due consideration will be given to the context, to the social and financial condition of the particular owner, and to question for how many others of his own day his particular case is typical. Other persons, from the few passages containing statistical evidence of doubtful worth, have developed a theoretical total, presumably applicable to any time throughout the two centuries. This total they have then endeavored to support by a limited number of quotations from the authors, paying little attention to the important economic changes during the period. But, as will be seen, it appears that no attempt has ever been made before this to reconstruct directly from the picture of Athenian society mirrored in the authors, with emphasis upon the economic conditions and the chronological factor, the possible number of slaves owned in Athens during the fifth and fourth centuries before Christ.[6]

[5]The following is the type of statement often made in a so-called "popular" article of a current magazine: "Its population [Attica] in its flourishing time was probably about 500,000 of which nearly four-fifths were slaves." *National Geographic Magazine*, (Dec., 1922), "Attica," 574.

[6]The method is essentially that which Letronne advocated more than one hundred years ago, although he himself apparently utilized only the passages which furnish statistical evidence: "Mais une lecture attentive des auteurs attiques m'a persuadé qu'on n'avoit pas tiré un assez grand parti des documents qu'ils contiennent et que la population de cette contrée à l'époque de sa plus grande splendeur n'avait pas été suffisamment établie."*Mém. de l'Acad. des Inscrip. et Belles-Lettres* 6, (1822), 168.

CHAPTER I

THE PRESENT STATUS OF THE PROBLEM

The few statistical passages which have served as a basis for the many involved discussions extending over a century and a half, I shall group here, for convenience, though each will be discussed at some length later in this chapter. There seems to be but one direct record regarding the total number of slaves in Athens. Athenaeus,[1] on the authority of a certain Ctesicles,[2] states that from a census taken by order of Demetrius Phalareus (probably about 309 b. c.) there were found to be in Attica 21,000 citizens, 10,000 metics, and 400,000 slaves.[3] In addition to this, a fragment from Hyperides,[4] which has come down to us in a mutilated condition, contributes an obscure statement which has been interpreted by some to mean that there were more than 150,000 slaves in the mines and in the rest of the country. To these passages may be added two noteworthy observations of Thucydides: the first, that Chios had more slaves than any state except Sparta;[5] the second, that the desertion of 20,000 slaves at the time of the occupation of Decelea by the Spartans brought the

---

[1]Athenaeus, VI, 272 c: Κτησικλῆς δ' ἐν τρίτῃ χρονικῶν <κατὰ τὴν ἑπτα> καιδεκάτην πρὸς ταῖς ἑκατόν φησιν ὀλυμπιάδα Ἀθήνησιν ἐξετασμὸν γενέσθαι ὑπὸ Δημητρίου τοῦ Φαληρέως τῶν κατοικούντων τὴν Ἀττικὴν καὶ εὑρεθῆναι Ἀθηναίους μὲν δισμυρίους πρὸς τοῖς χιλίοις, μετοίκους δὲ μυρίους, οἰκετῶν δὲ μυριάδας μ'.

[2]He is known only from this fragment and one other, also preserved by Athenaeus (X, 445d) alluding to the death of Eumenes. Both are quoted from the third book of his χρονικά.

[3]Athenaeus (VI, 272 b, d) also leaves us numbers for the slaves of Aegina and Corinth, about which there has been much discussion: . . κἂν τῇ τρίτῃ δὲ τῶν ἱστοριῶν ὁ Ἐπιτίμαιος ἔφη οὕτως εὐδαιμονῆσαι τὴν Κορινθίων πόλιν ὡς κτήσασθαι δούλων μυριάδας ἓξ καὶ τεσσαράκοντα. . . . Ἀριστοτέλης δ' ἐν Αἰγινητῶν πολιτείᾳ καὶ παρὰ τούτοις φησὶ γενέσθαι ἑπτὰ καὶ τεσσαράκοντα μυριάδας δούλων.

[4]Hyperides, c. Aristogeit., Frag. VII, 29 (Blass): ὅπως πρῶτον μὲν μυριάδας πλείους ἢ δεκαπέντε τοὺς <δούλους τοὺς> ἐκ τῶν ἔργων τῶν ἀργυρείων καὶ τοὺς κατὰ τὴν ἄλλην χώραν, ἔπειτα τοὺς ὀφείλοντας τῷ δημοσίῳ καὶ τοὺς ἀπεψηφισμένους καὶ τοὺς μετοίκους (Suid. [Bernh.] 1, 1 p. 562, 19).

[5]VIII, 40, 2: . . . οἱ γὰρ οἰκέται τοῖς Χίοις πολλοὶ ὄντες καὶ μιᾷ γε πόλει πλὴν Λακεδαιμονίων πλεῖστοι γενόμενοι καὶ ἅμα διὰ τὸ πλῆθος χαλεπωτέρως ἐν ταῖς ἀδικίαις κολαζόμενοι.

13

Athenians to great distress.[6] These bits of information have been subjected to all manner of criticism and interpretation during which many valuable data have been assembled.

David Hume was one of the first men to question seriously the testimony of Athenaeus. In an essay[7] entitled "Of the Populousness of Ancient Nations," published in 1752, in which he opposed the prevailing view that in antiquity there were fifty times as many people as in his own age, he ventured to assert:[8] "In my opinion, there is no point of criticism more certain than that Athenaeus and Ctesicles, whom he quotes, are here mistaken, and that the number of slaves [he refers here to adult male slaves] is at least augmented by a cipher and ought not to be regarded as more than 40,000."[9] He then proceeded to present ten objections to the number 400,000 for the slaves [adult male] of Athens. Because these have been the framework upon which later scholars have built more elaborate discussions, it is fitting to list them here with the mere mention of the proof adduced by Hume for each. First, 400,000 slaves[10] together with the free population would give Athens a larger population than London and Paris united, which is inconsistent with other data; secondly, there were but 10,000 houses[11] in Athens; thirdly, Xenophon[12] says that there was much empty space within the walls; fourthly, no insurrection of slaves or suspicion of insurrection is even mentioned by historians, except one commotion of the miners;[13] fifthly, the treatment of slaves by the Athenians is said to have been gentle and indulgent,[14] which would not have been the case had the disproportion been twenty to one; sixthly, Timarchus,[15] said to have been left in easy circum-

---

[6]VII, 27, 5: τῆς τε γὰρ χώρας ἁπάσης ἐστέρηντο, καὶ ἀνδραπόδων πλέον ἢ δύο μυριάδες ηὐτομοληκεσαν, καὶ τούτων τὸ πολὺ μέρος χειροτέχναι, κτλ.

[7]*Essays Moral, Political, and Literary* (London, 1752; Green and Grose ed. (1898), I, 381-443).

[8]I, 419 (Green and Grose ed.).

[9]The 40,000, in his opinion, would refer only to adult males, which number he multiplies by the coefficient of four to give a total slave population of 160,000.

[10]Hume is here reckoning the 400,000 as though it included only male slaves. But *v. infra*, 16 f.

[11]Xen., *Mem.*, III, 6, 14; *v. infra*, 63 f., note 92.

[12]*Vectigal.*, II, 6.

[13]Athen., VI, 272 f.; but *v. infra*, 93, note 37.

[14]Xen., *Pol. Ath.*, I, 10; Demosth., IX, 3; Plautus, *Stichus*, 446 ff.

[15]Aeschin., I, 97.

stances, owned only ten slaves employed in manufactures; Lysias[16]
and his brother, proscribed for their great riches, had only sixty
slaves apiece; Demosthenes, left rich by his father, owned no more
than fifty-two slaves;[17] seventhly, during the siege of Decelea the
desertion of 20,000 slaves brought the Athenians to great distress,[18]
which could not have happened had they been only the twentieth
part; eighthly, Xenophon[19] felt himself obliged to prove to his
readers that as large a number as 10,000 slaves could be successfully maintained by the state; ninthly, the valuation of property
for the whole state of Athens, as given by two authors,[20] was only
about 6,000 talents, with which it would be difficult to reconcile
even 40,000 slaves, i. e., adult males, which would imply a total, he
thinks, of 160,000, inasmuch as the lowest that Demosthenes[21]
estimates any of his father's slaves to be worth is two minas a
head; tenthly, Chios is said by Thucydides[22] to contain more slaves
than any Greek city except Sparta, a statement which, if Athens
had 400,000, would imply an incredibly large number for
Sparta, where at one time the murder of 2,000 Helots[23] was expected to weaken their strength, not merely to irritate them. In a
note[24] following the ten points, Hume added something which was
to be the center for much of the later research on this question:
"Also the Athenians brought yearly from the Pontus 400,000
medimni of corn, as appeared from the custom-house books.[25]
And this was the greater part of their importation. Now this is
strong proof that there is some mistake in the foregoing passage
of Athenaeus, for Attica was so barren it could not maintain its
peasants,[26] and 400,000 medimni would scarcely feed 100,000 a
year."

Such is the outline of the problem as stated by Hume and, inad-
equately supported as some of the arguments are, the list is very

[16]Lysias, XII, 19.
[17]Demosth., XXVII, 9.
[18]Thucyd., VII, 27.
[19]Vectigal., IV, 25.
[20]Demosth., XIV, 19; Polybius, II, 62.
[21]XXVII, 9.
[22]VIII, 40.
[23]Thucyd., IV, 80.
[24]Op. cit., I, 421 (Green and Grose ed.).
[25]Demosth., XX, 32.
[26]Livy, XLIII, 6.

nearly complete. He refers to it, himself, as "an essay merely starting some doubts, scruples, and difficulties sufficiently to make us suspend our judgment on that head."[27] But it is much more than that, it is, in fact, the outline for all future investigations into the problem of the slave population of Attica. That he, so early in the problem, with so little philological training, had the vision to accomplish this is remarkable. As we proceed in our summary of the results of later researches, we shall constantly need to refer to Hume's ten arguments in order to see what has been added to the proof or disproof of each, thus measuring each man's contribution to the subject.

Following Hume and amplifying his proof, in addition to introducing into the discussion a statement from Xenophon[28] about theoretical plans for the mines, Letronne still further reduced the number of slaves from 160,000 to 120,000. His work has been analyzed and evaluated by Wallon, who will be mentioned later.[29] Robert Wallace[30] and Ste. Croix,[31] in answer to Hume, defended the number of slaves recorded by Athenaeus. But it was reserved for August Boeckh[32] in his well-known work *Die Staatshaushaltung der Athener* to attempt a refutation of Hume's statements that has become almost standard among all later defenders of the view that Athenian civilization rested mainly on slavery. Because his conclusions have been since incorporated into so many articles, it will be necessary to examine more closely than in other cases upon what grounds they rest, especially those which bring corrections or additional information to the ten arguments formulated by Hume.

Hume's first point, that the number of slaves mentioned in the census of Demetrius referred only to adult males, since the 21,000 citizens and the 10,000 metics mentioned in the passage were clearly of that class, is correctly attacked by Boeckh. The latter satisfactorily explains that slaves were of course regarded like any other possession and like cattle reckoned by heads; therefore,

---

[27]*Op. cit.*, Intro. I, 56 (Green and Grose ed.).

[28]Xen., *Vectigal.*, IV, 17 f., *v. infra*, 25 and 88 f.

[29]*V. infra*, 25 ff.

[30]*Dissertation on the Numbers of Mankind*, etc., (Edinburgh, 1753).

[31]"Mémoire sur la Population de L'Attique," *Mém. de Litt. des Inscrip. et Belles-Lettres*, 48 (1808), 147 ff.   I owe this and the preceding reference to Wallon.

[32]1st ed. (1817), 2nd ed. (1850), 3rd ed. by Fränkel (1886), 47 ff.

there would be no sense in omitting any part of their total number in a census. The truth of this correction has been with one exception[33] generally acknowledged ever since. But I cannot accept Boeckh's next correction. In his opinion, the 400,000 is a round number with several thousand added on for good measure. Hence he arbitrarily reduces it to 365,000 in all later computations. This is a surprisingly large reduction. Why rob the Athenians of 35,000 slaves with one stroke of the pen? We know that great financial distress ensued when only 20,000 ran away to Decelea.[34]

The second point, namely, that there were only 10,000 houses in Athens,[35] Boeckh does not question, although he finds it difficult to find roofs to shelter all the population, since Xenophon[36] left the information that for one house fourteen free members was a large number. But he finally puts the surplus in the lodging houses (συνοικίαι), while the factories (Fabrikhaüser), he says, provided for many hundreds of slaves.[37]

To meet Hume's third contention that the city appears not to have been densely populated to any extraordinary degree, since Xenophon asserts that there were many vacant lots in the city, Boeckh[38] with some difficulty arbitrarily distributes the population of 500,000 throughout Attica as follows: in the sixty and one-fourth square miles which he accepts as the area of the city and of the mining district together, he assigns 180,000 to the former and 60,000 to the latter. For the rest of the state (749¼ square miles according to his reckoning) he allows 260,000. In a district as proverbially barren as Attica,[39] this average of 617 persons to the square mile[40] is simply incredible. Boeckh admits

[33]Beloch, *v. infra*, 32.

[34]Thucyd., VII, 27.

[35]In the third edition of Boeckh's work, vol. II, see Fränkel's note 77, p. 11, concerning this as evidence. Also, *v. infra*, 63 f. note 92.

[36]Xen., *Mem.*, II, 7, 2.

[37]I, 52 (3rd ed.). But *cf.* Bolkestein, *Fabrieken en Fabrikanten in Griekenland*, p. 16.

[38]*Op. cit.*, 52 f.

[39]Aeschyl., *Pers.*, 790 ff.

[40]This would require us to picture it as almost six times as densely populated as the state of Delaware where there is an average of 113.5 persons for each of the 1,965 square miles of land. It represents Attica with its rocky hillsides and barren soil as considerably more thickly settled than Rhode Island whose population is 97.5% urban in composition yet averages only 566.4 to the square mile. (*Statistical Abstract of the United States* (1921), 1, 50 f., 54.)

(p. 52), "Eine grosse Menge von Lebensmitteln aber erforderte diese Bevölkerung allerdings," but he reassures us: "indess darf nicht ausser Acht gelassen werden, dass Sklaven schlecht genährt wurden, und vorzüglich nur Getreidezufuhr erforderlich war."

The facts that slaves were mildly treated at Athens, and that no insurrections are recorded, are passed over in silence. But, opposing Hume's belief that the testimony of literature tended to show that even the wealthiest men had no very large number of slaves, Boeckh maintains (p. 49) that there were, on the average, at least four slaves to every free man, woman, or child in Athens. Here it is pertinent to note exactly what literary evidence is assembled, for this is the *locus classicus*[41] from which so many have long been quoting that it would seem that many writers on this subject have looked for their information about slavery among the Greeks to Boeckh and not to Greek literature.

"Even a poor citizen kept a slave to care for his house (*cf.* the beginning of Aristophanes' *Plutus*).[42] In every important establishment many of them were used for all sorts of possible occupations, such as grinders, bakers, cooks, tailors, errand boys, and to accompany master and mistress who seldom went out without an escort. Anyone who was prosperous and wished to attract attention took, perhaps, three attendants with him.[43] Even philosophers were found with ten slaves. Slaves were also let out as hired servants; they performed the labor connected with the care of cattle and agriculture; they were employed in the working of mines and furnaces; all manual labor and the lower branches of trade were in a great measure carried on by them; whole hosts worked in the numerous work shops for which Athens was noted; a great number in the merchant ships and navy. To pass over several examples of those who owned a smaller number, Timarchus[44] had eleven or twelve in his workshop, Demosthenes' father fifty-two or -three without the slave women in his house,[45] Lysias

---

[41] I, 49 (3rd ed.).

[42] But *cf.* Beloch's remark (*Die Bevölkerung der Griechisch-Römischen Welt*, 92): "Armuth ist eben ein sehr relativer Begriff; und wenn der Chremylos des Plutos auch kein reicher Mann ist, so ist er doch noch lange kein Proletarier." *V. infra*, 77 f.

[43] Demosth., XXXVI, 45. But *v. infra*, 45, note 14.

[44] Aeschin., I, 97.

[45] Demosth., XXVII, 9; 46.

and Polemarchus one hundred twenty.[46] That frequently a free man had fifty slaves, a rich man still more, Plato remarks expressly.[47] And then Philemonides had 300, Hipponicus 600, and Nicias 1,000 employed in the mines alone.[48] These facts prove a large number of slaves."[49]

But, just how large a slave population do these statements prove? Not a passage is cited from ancient literature to inform us of the numbers used in all trades, agriculture, and so forth. That "ganze Schaaren" worked in the "zahlreichen Werkstätte" is not supported by any proof offered. As for the individuals cited as slave-owners, we can prove but little by them unless they are typical Athenian citizens. Who are these seven who are mentioned? It is enough for the present to note that Hipponicus with the 600 slaves was rated as the richest man of his time,[50] and was the son of Callias,[51] the richest man of the preceding generation. Nicias[52] was one of the very few men of his age who had 100 talents of property. At a time when probably only 1,200 of 21,000 citizens possessed three talents or more,[53] Demosthenes' father[54] had fourteen talents. Though Lysias[55] and Polemarchus were proscribed for their wealth by the Thirty, they had only sixty slaves apiece. Timarchus[56] inherited a considerable sum of money from his father besides two estates from his uncles and spent it all lavishly, while there is reason to believe that Philemonides[57] was a very wealthy man. These, then, are the richest men for a period of seventy-five years in Athens. Their average of almost 300 slaves apiece would have to be equalled by hundreds of their contemporaries to bring the total up to 365,000 slaves in Attica.

[46]Lys., XII, 19.

[47]Plato, *Resp.*, IX, 578 D, E. Beloch quite justly remarks (*op. cit.*, 93, note): "Böckh hat sich erlaubt das Zeugnis zu fälschen indem er sagt: dass bei einem freien Manne. . . etc." *Cf.* also the misuse of this evidence by Saco in his otherwise sane discussion (*Historia de la Esclavitud*, I, 163).

[48]Xen., *Vectigal.*, IV, 14 ff.

[49]I, 49 f. (3rd ed.). In chapters 2, 3, and 4 below this evidence is more fully discussed.

[50]Andocides, I, 130; Lys., XIX, 48.

[51]Plut., *Aristid.*, 25.

[52]Lysias, XIX, 48.

[53]*V. infra*, 105.

[54]Demosth., XXVII, 11.

[55]Lysias, XII, 19.

[56]Aeschin., I, 101; 116.

[57]Xen., *Vectigal.*, IV, 15.

To the seventh and eighth points raised by Hume, namely, that there could have been no great number of slaves if the flight of 20,000 to Decelea caused distress, and if Xenophon also felt that an increase of 10,000 was important enough to have to be justified, Boeckh rejoins that after the Decelean experience perhaps the people did not acquire many slaves on account of the facility of escape, or might even have dismissed some. But, he rather lamely adds: "the passage in Xenophon is strangely incoherent and therefore, should not be used as a basis for conclusions."[58]

The statements also recorded by Athenaeus, that Corinth had 460,000 and Aegina 470,000 slaves, are considered by Boeckh to be exaggerated but not impossible, for the Corinthians were often called χοινικομέτραι (measurers of the χοῖνιξ, the daily ration of slaves),[59] and Aegina, he says, though only about forty square miles in area, could not possibly have been a great business city and important naval power, as she was, without a large population and a great number of slaves. But such a large number, he thinks, is to be inferred only for earlier times, that is, before Athens gained the supremacy.[60]

Boeckh passes over Thucydides' remark that Chios[61] had more slaves than any state except the Lacedaemonian, but in his second edition (1850) he introduces a bit of evidence which was to be the point of contention in many a discussion since: the ambiguous statement of Hyperides,[62] that there were 150,000 slaves in the mines and in the rest of the country: ὅπως πρῶτον μὲν μυριάδας πλείους ἢ δεκαπέντε τοὺς < δούλους τοὺς > ἐκ τῶν ἔργων τῶν ἀργυρείων καὶ τοὺς κατὰ τὴν ἄλλην χώραν, κτλ. From this we are to infer, in Boeckh's opinion (p. 48 and note a, 3rd ed.), that besides the slaves in the city, previously reckoned, as it would appear, there were in the country, including the mines, 150,000 adult male slaves. With the 50,000, which is his estimate of those in the city, the total would be over 200,000 adult males, leaving the smaller half of the recorded 400,000 for women and children.

---

[58]I, 51 (3rd ed.).

[59]Athen., VI, 272 b, d.

[60]This would allow an average of almost twelve thousand slaves, to say nothing of the masters, to every square mile of this barren, rocky isle. *V. infra*, 31 f.

[61]VIII, 40, 2.

[62]Hyperides, *c. Aristog.*, fr. VII, 29 (Blass). *V. supra*, 16.

But we had granted Boeckh at the beginning that slaves were not listed separately according to sex or age in an enumeration, so why should we suppose that Hyperides listed only the adult men? Besides, there is no reason for believing positively that the words κατὰ τὴν ἄλλην χώραν exclude the city,[63] nor in believing that a separate count of city slaves was made in connection with the free citizens. For a writer so scrupulous as to object to basing conclusions on Xenophon's remark about the 10,000 in the mines, it is singular that he should place so much credence in his interpretation of this doubtful passage. It has, moreover, come down to us in such a mutilated condition that I agree with the others who will be mentioned later that it should be either interpreted differently or else discarded altogether as evidence.[64]

More specific is the argument adduced against the figure of approximately 6,000 talents as the valuation of property in Attica. This is a very important obstacle for anyone to surmount who believes that the slaves at Athens numbered several hundreds of thousands, because, as has been stated before, this amount stands well attested by ancient authorities.[65] But Boeckh

[63]Ciccotti (Del numero, etc., 657) answers Boeckh effectively on this point. His argument, in brief, is that, as Hyperides was speaking of a general levy to meet the imminent Macedonian army, before mentioning the total of fighting men among the slaves it would have been appropriate, as he did, to give the total number. Χώρα may mean country in general, including city. Boeckh, in his opinion, only through the necessity of establishing the number 365,000, imagined that those in the city had been listed elsewhere, perhaps with the citizens.

[64]V. infra, 36.

[65]Polyb., II, 62, 6: τίς γὰρ ὑπὲρ Ἀθηναίων οὐχ ἱστόρηκε διότι καθ' οὓς καιροὺς μετὰ Θηβαίων εἰς τὸν πρὸς Λακεδαιμονίους ἐνέβαινον πόλεμον . . . ὅτι τότε κρίναντες ἀπὸ τῆς ἀξίας ποιεῖσθαι τὰς εἰς τὸν πόλεμον εἰσφορὰς ἐτιμήσαντο τὴν τε χώραν τὴν Ἀττικὴν ἅπασαν καὶ τὰς οἰκίας, ὁμοίως δὲ καὶ τὴν λοιπὴν οὐσίαν · ἀλλ' ὅμως τὸ σύμπαν τίμημα τῆς ἀξίας ἐνέλιπε τῶν ἑξακισχιλίων διακοσίοις καὶ πεντήκοντα ταλάντοις. "Who has not read that when the Athenians, in conjunction with the Thebans, entered on the war against Sparta (378/7 B. C.), sending out a force of ten thousand men and manning a hundred triremes, they decided to meet the war expenses by a property tax and made a valuation for this purpose of the whole of Attica including the houses and other property. This estimate, however, fell short of 6,000 talents by 250 . . ." (Paton's transl.). Demosthenes in the speech delivered 354/3 B. C. (XIV, 19) gives the valuation in round numbers as 6000 talents: . . ἐπειδὴ τὸ τίμημ' ἐστὶ τῆς χώρας ἑξακισχιλίων ταλάντων and refers to the same amount again in this speech (XIV, 30). Harpocration (s. v. ὅτι ἑξακιχίλιοι) preserves this remark of Demosthenes and adds the information that Philochorus also declared that the valuation of property in Attica was 6,000 talents (Philochorus, fr. 151, Müller, I, 409).

argues[66] that such a valuation of property, exclusive of state-owned and religious possessions, must not represent its actual value. The amount of land which he has assumed to be devoted to grain in Attica would be worth 7,500 talents alone, and the 365,000 slaves he thinks would be worth at the minimum 6,000 talents. How, then, could the Athenians themselves have valued their property at only 5,750 talents? In spite of the definite statement to the contrary, he thinks that this figure must have represented only a fixed portion of the property, since the total amount taxable must have been 20,000 talents and the real total between 30,000 and 40,000 talents (p. 577).

But if only 20,000 talents of this sum are reckoned as property paying interest, each of the 20,000 citizens would have had the interest of a talent or an annual income (at twelve percent) of 720 drachmas[67] . . So it would be interesting to know just who did own the property, for at that time a fortune of 200 talents was almost unknown and a man with fourteen talents (the father of Demosthenes) was reckoned as one of the richest in Athens.[68] What Beloch and Grote have said against the possibility of inferring such a high valuation for Attica, as Boeckh does, will be discussed below.[69]

To provide a total population of 500,000 in Attica with sufficient food, which meant in those days largely wheat and barley, required a great effort. Relying upon Boeckh's estimate of the amount of grain that Attica, although proverbially a barren country, could raise, and his estimate of the amount imported, based upon a statement of Demosthenes, later writers have made frequent use of the probable amount of the consumption of grain as a main prop in the defense of a large slave population for Attica. It is worth while, therefore, to outline Boeckh's treatment of this argument.

Demosthenes had stated that 400,000 medimni of grain were imported from the Pontus yearly, and that it was an amount

---

[66]*Op. cit.*, I, 571 ff. (3rd ed.).

[67]At that time 360 drachmas a year comfortably supported a family of four. *Cf.* Busolt, *Griechische Staatskunde* (1920), 203, 4.

[68]*V. infra*, 97.

[69]*V. infra*, 33.

nearly equal to Athens' whole importation from other countries.[70] Boeckh[71] begins then by doubling this 400,000 medimni, but adds an extra 200,000 medimni because Demosthenes, being an orator, could have modified the truth a little and might not have had accurate information, even if he did invoke the books of the σιτοφύλακες as proof. Thus he reaches a total importation of 1,000,000 medimni a year. Next, he computes the average amount consumed in a year by each individual. That a slave had one choenix a day allotted to him is generally agreed.[72] In a year of 354 days this would amount to seven and three-fourths medimni apiece, but, allowing for children, he estimates that there would be a yearly average of about six medimni for each, or a total of 810,000 medimni for 135,000 free citizens and 2,607,500 medimni for 365,000 slaves, that is 3,400,000 medimni for all, without counting the amount required for seed. By further calculations and comparison with Sicily and other countries, he decides that one plethron might have yielded on the average two and five-eighths medimni and allowing one-seventh as necessary for sowing, 1,066,657 plethra (but v. infra, 82) would be necessary to produce 2,800,000 medimni each year. By this estimate, 1,237,333 plethra would be left in Attica for swamps, forests, vineyards, fallow land, grazing, space for dwellings, and so forth. Boeckh himself admits that the fact that Phaenippus' estate of 3200 plethra[73] produced only 1,000 medimni of grain in one year is rather unfavorable to this reckoning, but he thinks that this does not prove the conclusions to be inadmissible.[74]

Unfortunately for these conclusions, the only inscriptional evidence that has come to light completely refutes them. Not merely does Phaenippus' farm, whatever its area, and there is considerable doubt upon that point, show that the estimate of such a large yield of grain was improbable, but the actual figures for the

---

[70]XX, 31: πρὸς τοίνυν ἄπαντα τὸν ἐκ τῶν ἄλλων ἐμπορίων ἀφικνούμενον ὁ ἐκ τοῦ Πόντου σῖτος εἰσπλέων ἐστίν . . . αἱ τοίνυν παρ' ἐκείνου δεῦρ' ἀφικνούμεναι σίτου μυριάδες περὶ τετταράκοντ' εἰσί · καὶ τοῦτ' ἐκ τῆς παρὰ τοῖς σιτοφύλαξιν ἀπογραφῆς ἄν τις ἴδοι.

[71]Op. cit., I, 100 ff. (3rd ed.).

[72]Herodot., VII, 187; Diog. Laert., VIII, 18; Thucyd., IV, 16; VII, 87; cf. Busolt, op. cit., 202.

[73]Demosth., XLII, 5; 20.

[74]Op. cit., I, 102 (3rd ed.).

year 329/8 B. C. recorded in an inscription at Eleusis[75] which lists the gifts of barley and wheat to the two goddesses furnish us the means of reckoning almost exactly the entire wheat and barley crop by tribes in Attica for that year. It was not 2,000,000 medimni nor one-half, nor one-third of that, but only 400,000. This year, as well as the few just preceding, *may* have been one with abnormally poor harvests, as Foucart points out, but even on that quite gratuitous assumption, this must represent from one-half to one-fourth of the usual crop, which would still be far from Boeckh's estimate.[76]

It might be well to inquire now what has been accomplished by Boeckh and his many followers, important among whom were Clinton[77] and Büchsenschütz,[78] toward the solution of this problem concerning the slave population. To sum it up briefly, the number 400,000 reduced arbitrarily to 365,000 is shown to indicate a total number of slaves, not adult males only; the questionable testimony of Hyperides about the 150,000 in the mines and the rest of the country is introduced into the discussion; a definitely restricted amount of literary evidence is cited in an effort to prove the preponderance of slave labor, and ambitious attempts are made to prove that the actual amount of property in Attica was between 30,000 and 40,000 talents, and that the grain production was about 2,800,000 medimni yearly. It was left for later investigators definitely to establish the untenability of most of these views, to reduce the number 400,000 permanently, and to emphasize the importance of free labor, without, however, reaching any agreement as to the actual number of slaves in Attica.

[75]*I. G.*, IV², 834b, II.

For a discussion of this inscription see: Foucart, "Note sur les Comptes d'Eleusis," *Bull. de Corr. Hell.*, 8 (1884), 194-216. Lycurgus appears to have revived the practice instituted by Pericles, of dedicating 1/600 of the barley and 1/1200 of the wheat raised in Athens and the cleruchies to Demeter and her daughter. The inscription gives the total of this thank-offering by tribes.

[76]Fränkel, the editor of the third edition of Boeckh's work, expresses some concern as to the unfavorable light which this inscription throws upon Boeckh's calculations (*op. cit.*, II, 22,* note 142).

[77]Clinton, *Fasti Hellenici* (1841), II, 479-82.

[78]Büchsenschütz, *Besitz und Erwerb* (1869), 137-42. *Cf.* also Moreau de Jonnés, *Statistique des Peuples de l'Antiquité* (Paris, 1851), 178 ff.

Wallon[79] took the next forward step in the study of this subject, following to some extent and revising considerably Letronne's scheme of presentation. After a detailed treatment of each topic, he says that he believes that he has proved:[80] 1. That the number of 60,000 slaves alluded to by Xenophon[81] when he proposes to buy slaves to work in the mines until the number equals three for each citizen can give no conclusion relative to the total number in Attica, since it referred only to mines, and was, besides, purely theory.[82] 2. That the number 400,000 in Athenaeus[83] is a round number including not adult males but all the servile population. 3. That the statement of Thucydides[84] relative to the servile population of Chios and Laconia, of which the latter probably had 220,000 Helots, would justify us in conjecturing that Chios had about 210,000 and that hence Athens' servile population could not have much surpassed 200,000. It is not necessary to give the details here of the proof of the second point, for the essential elements have been discussed in the summary of Boeckh's work, but we must pause to see upon what grounds Wallon feels so certain that the number 400,000 should be cut in two, but not reduced to the 120,000 reached by the calculations of Letronne.

Thucydides' reference (VIII, 40, 2) to Chios is made the basis of the whole discussion:[85] "Now the Chians had more domestic slaves than any other state with the exception of Lacedaemon, and their offences were always more severely punished because of their number" (Jowett's transl.). From this Wallon argues that Sparta had the most slaves, Chios was next, while Athens very likely stood third. To translate this statement of Thucydides into a numerical estimate is a more difficult task for him. But

[79]*Histoire de l'Esclavage dans l'Antiquité* (1847, 2nd ed., 1879), I, 220-83 (2nd ed.).

[80]*Op. cit.*, I, 275 (2nd ed.).

[81]*Vectigal.*, IV, 17 f. *V. infra*, 88.

[82]This was in answer to Letronne (*v. supra*, 16) who had emphasized this statement together with the chance remark of the banqueter (Athen., VI, 272 e) that the myriads of slaves just mentioned in the figures reported from Demetrius' census were for the most part employed in the mines. As this argument has been of little importance in the discussions of the question, Letronne's treatment of it and Wallon's refutation are dismissed with this mention.

[83]VI, 272 c.

[84]VIII, 40, 2; *v. supra*, 13.

[85]*Op. cit.*, I, 231 ff. (2nd ed.).

from some remarks of Herodotus[86] regarding conditions in Sparta about 480 B. C., he concludes that the number of Helots in 412 B. C. was about 220,000. Furthermore, because Thucydides refers to the wealth and general importance of the Chians (I, 116, 117; II, 56; IV, 31), Wallon infers that their number of slaves could not have been other than about 10,000 less than those which he has secured for Sparta, or 210,000. The number which must have been in Athens, he adds, confirms this estimate of 210,000 for Chios. By such a series of guesses is the figure obtained which must be used as the upper limit for the slave population at Athens! The next step in Wallon's discussion, the attempt to establish the number of approximately 200,000 slaves in Attica, is the most significant for this particular study, for he states that he intends to prove the correctness of this estimate by citing the texts of the historians, comic poets, and orators, by calculating the number in the different lines of work, and lastly by meeting all objections that might be raised.[87]

He first attempts to compute carefully the probable number of slaves in household service. From twenty-five passages cited from a wide range of authors dealing with people of different social position, he finds that slaves, especially women, were commonly employed in Athenian households. He then reckons that every family, or rather house, in Athens had slaves so employed. From two statements by Xenophon he believes that there were 10,000 houses[88] in Athens, while in the Piraeus and the numerous market

[86]It might be well to point out in passing, although the question, strictly speaking, does not fall within the province of this present study, that this upper limit of 220,000 commonly accepted as the number of Helots in Sparta rests, after all, upon very slight evidence. Herodotus records that Sparta had 8,000 citizens capable of military training (VII, 234), and again that she sent 5,000 citizens each of them accompanied by seven Helots to fight at Plataea (IX, 10, 28). Mainly upon these statements, Wallon (111 ff.) reckons the total free population as 31,400 and assumes seven Helots for each or a total of 220,000. More than this, the figures thus obtained for the time of the battle of Plataea (about 480 B. C.) are regarded as applicable to the time to which Thucydides had reference (412 B. C.).

[87]Op. cit., I, 234-45 (2nd ed.).

[88]Xen., Mem., III, 6, 14. See Beloch (op. cit., 100, note 2), Wachsmuth (Stadt Athen, I, 564, note 2), and Busolt (op. cit., 199) who believe that οἰκίαι is shown by the context to mean households, not houses. V. infra, 63 and supra, 14, 17. Xen., Oec., VIII, 22, which Wallon (241) cites in support of 10,000 houses for Athens, contains no evidence on the subject.

towns there might have been 10,000 more. (See Chapter II[89] of this study for more complete discussion of this point.) It would appear reasonable then to Wallon to reckon two for each of these houses or 40,000 for domestic service.

To estimate the number employed on the farms seems to have been far less troublesome for Wallon. Fewer than five passages, none of them directly mentioning slaves, lead him to infer that the number of Athenians engaged in agriculture was very large, that the 15,000 or 16,000 who owned land, of course, had slaves to make it more productive, and that the care of the vineyards, olive orchards, grain land, and cattle could easily have employed on an average two for each land-owner or 30,000 to 40,000, say 35,000.[90]

An example of how scholars not infrequently appear to have decided in advance what was the proportion of slave labor to free, and then by means of literature to have tried to find that number, is this particular use of such scanty literary evidence to prove the existence of 35,000 slaves. From the statement of Dionysius Hal., *Lysias*, 32, (=Lysias, XXXIV, argumentum) that, after the overthrow of the Thirty, 5,000 were threatened with losing the rights of citizenship because of their owning no land, Wallon claims that there is shown that 15,000 or 16,000 citizens not only owned land but had at least two slaves apiece with which to till it. Besides, he adds, there were extensive domains in addition to the small land-holdings, as one can infer from Demosthenes' oration against Leptines,[91] in which it would appear that Leucon owned extensive property in Attica. Also Xenophon in a few chapters of the *Oeconomicus*[92] shows us in Ischomachus, "all degrees of commanding and obedience: a double hierarchy that presupposes a numerous household." This is every bit of evidence brought forward in determining the number of slaves employed in agriculture!

But the total is still too small. There are yet 125,000 slaves to be discovered somewhere. Most of these are to be found in the

[89]*V. infra*, 63 and note 92.

[90]*Op. cit.*, I, 246.

[91]XX, 40. There is nothing in the passage to warrant that interpretation. The exact words are: χρήματα μὲν γάρ ἐστιν ἀεὶ παρ' ὑμῖν αὐτοῦ. This money referred to was, no doubt, invested in shipping enterprises.

[92]VII, IX, XI to XVI. See below, 69 ff. for a discussion of the household of Ischomachus.

different branches of industry or commerce. For the mines and quarries, Wallon regards as acceptable Letronne's[93] estimate of 10,000, found by a comparison of the known revenues of certain mines with the probable revenue of the mines of Laurion. The fact, moreover, that Xenophon, in his dreams of filling the state treasury with an income derived from state-owned slaves, limits the experiment at first to 10,000 may indicate in Wallon's opinion a number known to be employed there at that time. For other industries, important conclusions are drawn from the eight passages cited as representative of conditions in Athens. These mention the dozen slaves owned by Timarchus,[94] the fifty-three who belonged to the father of Demosthenes,[95] the slave workmen whom Leocrates owned,[96] Euctemon's slaves,[97] "the numerous slaves counted on the rolls of population, but scattered over the seas of the Greek world,"[98] those owned by metics, as the 120 of Lysias and Polemarchus,[99] and the slaves for hire mentioned by Isaeus[100] and Demosthenes.[101] With the first conclusion from this evidence we can agree, namely, that industry and commerce do not always require the same number of hands and that, accordingly, numbers were kept at a minimum by hiring additional slaves whenever there was need of extra help. But, on the basis of these few passages, of which only four mention definite numbers, we cannot be certain of the second conclusion, namely, that one can estimate three slaves for each Athenian citizen and metic old enough to employ them, or 90,000 employed in industry and commerce, exclusive of the mines.[102]

To estimate the number of children under twelve is more difficult since the servile class seems to have been recruited not so much from natural increase as from purchase. Wallon thinks, on the basis of evidence for women in domestic work, that we may

---

[93]*Op. cit.*, 211 ff.
[94]Aeschin., I, 97.
[95]Demosth., XXVII, 9.
[96]Lycurgus, *c.*, *Leocr.*, 58. No numbers are given.
[97]Isaeus, VI, 33. No numbers are given.
[98][Xen.] *Pol. Ath.*, I, 11. These are alluded to only vaguely.
[99]Lysias, XII, 19.
[100]Isaeus, VIII, 35.
[101]Demosth., XXVII, 20 f.
[102]Wallon, *op. cit.*, I, 249-51.

safely estimate 30,000 women for the homes and 10,000 for the factories and on the farms. There might not have been 40,000 married couples, but with the great license and corruption[103] and the number of children mentioned in the wills of Lycon[104] and Aristotle,[105] slave children, he thinks, could not have been much fewer than those born of free parents. The ratio of population in France[106] gave 29,000 children for 40,000 women, hence it seems plausible to him to assume for Attica 20,000 slaves under twelve years of age.[107] As for those over seventy, who Wallon seems to think would not be counted elsewhere, by the same law of population, allowing one for every thirty-two between twenty and sixty years of age, there would be 6,000. Therefore, concludes Wallon, the total number of slaves in Attica will be 201,000, almost exactly what he had previously estimated from Thucydides' chance remark that Chios had more slaves than Sparta! Applying the same law of population again, and using the average of 20,000 citizens and 10,000 metics, he finds that there would be a total population in Attica of 310,000 or 122 to the square kilometre.

The objection raised solely by Letronne, namely, that so great a number could not be maintained in time of war, is then met by emphasizing the large number of garrisons in Attica, and by referring to Xenophon's[108] statement that slaves were of great value during times of war in manning ships and filling armies. But it is not so easy to refute the objection that it would be difficult to provide food for so many thousands. For this we must again enter into the question of grain consumption.[109] Letronne's average of five and five-eighths medimni per person yearly is accepted (p. 260) as well as seventy-five stades or 2700 plethra as the area of the estate belonging to Phaenippus. From Aldenhoven's map (1838) Attica is shown to have not the 53,000 stades used by Letronne, but 70,048, or including Salamis, as seems proper, the total area would be 74,016 stades. If Phaenippus' estate produced 1,000 medimni of grain a year, then, says Wallon, the relative

[103][Xen.] *Pol. Ath.*, I, 11, *cf.*, *Oec.*, IX, 5.
[104]Diog. Laert., V, 4, 9.
[105]Diog. Laert., V, 1, 9.
[106]*L'Annuaire du Bureau des Longitudes* (1842).
[107]See Chapter VI of this study.
[108]Xen., *Vectigal.*, IV, 41-43.
[109]Wallon, *op. cit.*, 257 ff.

areas being in the proportion of 1:973, Attica and Salamis could easily produce 973,000 medimni. This, with the 1,000,000 medimni (p. 262) imported (accepted from Boeckh's figures), is 42,000 more than would be necessary to feed 310,000 inhabitants. To be sure, this quantity raised upon an estimated one-fifth of the area of the country is far more reasonable than Boeckh's 2,800,000 medimni upon approximately one-half of the surface of Attica. But to state, as Wallon does (p. 277), that this is one of the poorest grain crops imaginable for Attica,[110] is unfortunate in the light of the inscriptional evidence referred to before for the year 329/8 B.C.[111] Letronne's reckoning of a total yield of 486,000 medimni is much nearer the 400,000 medimni there recorded.

Based chiefly on Thucydides' remark that Chios had more slaves than any state except the Lacedemonian, and considerable straining of literary evidence, Wallon's conclusion that the slave population of Attica was 201,000 is, as a whole, unconvincing.

Richter,[112] as others before him, with no consideration of the amount of free labor that existed, accepts Wallon's system of grouping the slaves by classes, but, in order to obtain the number 400,000, which he states at the outset that he is interested in defending, increases certain groups with no justification. The 90,000 in industry, the 6,000 over seventy years of age, the 35,000 in agriculture, he takes without question, but upon the vaguest kind of testimony[113] the 40,000 in household service are increased to 100,000, and the 10,000 of the mines to 50,000. Worst of all, the public slaves "and so forth," whom Wallon did not add in at all, are set at 50,000 (p. 99) without a single reason being given for that number. Because of the general lack of thoroughness of this

---

[110]Demosth., XLII, 5; 20. Boeckh had reckoned the area of this farm as 3200 plethra (op. cit., I, 80). V. infra, chapter III, especially pages 71 f., for a discussion of this border-estate belonging to Phaenippus.

[111]V. supra, 23.

[112]Die Sklaverei im Griechischen Altertume (1886), 92 ff.

[113]The total evidence cited is: Aristoph., Eccles., 593. (Praxagora outlines a scheme whereby the unfairness of some having many slaves and others only one will be eliminated.) Aristot., Polit., II, 1, 10 (in families many attendants are often less useful than few); Plut., Apophth. reg., 175d. (Xenophanes complains that he can barely maintain two slaves.); Aeschines, Epist., XII (he says: "here I sit with seven slaves."), v. infra, 56, note 69; Plato, Resp., IX, 578 (refers to rich men with fifty slaves).

chapter on "Die Zahl der Sklaven," it makes very little difference, in any serious consideration of the subject, if Richter does shortly reach the conclusion that there were 100,000 in the households, in round numbers 100,000 in industry (that is 10,000 more than he has just accepted from Wallon), 150,000 in the mines and on the farms (assumed from the statement of Hyperides), while the other 50,000 might be taken as the state-owned slaves, and so forth; or as he sums it up (p. 99): "not only do we not doubt that the number of slaves recorded by Demetrius was *voll und ganz* in Attica, but we do not shrink from stating that, from the end of the Persian War to the beginning of the Peloponnesian War, they were still more numerous." Richter's defense of the numbers given in Athenaeus for the slaves in Corinth and Aegina (p. 99) is too slight to be worth even summarizing.

A notable advance was marked by Beloch in his *Bevölkerung der Griechisch-Römischen Welt,* for his estimates of population are based upon a computation of areas and a thorough-going analysis of literary evidence. He turns his attention first[114] to the only definite numbers left us for Attica: Demetrius' census. The figures of 21,000[115] for the adult citizens and 10,000 for the metics are accepted as probably correct because of their agreement with other substantial data, but the figures for the slaves of Aegina, Corinth, and Athens, as preserved in Athenaeus are shown from every point of view to be unworthy of belief.

For example, the island of Aegina with but approximately thirty-five square miles of surface on which 6,646 inhabitants were living in 1879 (approximately 8,000 now)[116] would have required, in Beloch's opinion, only a few thousand workmen to cultivate the rocky ground; at least 460,000 out of the 470,000 would necessarily, then, have been concentrated in the principal settlement, thus making Aegina incomparably the largest Greek city, in fact, three times as large as Periclean Athens. But the evidence[117] that Beloch has assembled elsewhere shows that Ath-

---

[114]*Op. cit.,* 57, 84 ff. *V. supra,* 13.

[115]However, in a later article ("Griechische Aufgebote," *Klio* 5, (1905) 341-74), Beloch (p. 366) is of the opinion that this 21,000 represented only those of military age, or a total of 25,000 citizens. This he promises to establish in a later discussion. *V. infra,* 34.

[116]*Handbook of Greece* (1920), I, 396.

[117]*Op. cit.,* 100; *cf.* Thucyd., IV, 95; I, 80; Xen., *Hellen.,* II, 3, 24.

ens was believed to be the largest city of Greece at that period. As for relegating hordes to Aegina's merchant ships, as some have suggested, this cannot be done, says Beloch (p. 84), because such vessels were propelled by sail and not by oars. The free population estimated at 2,000-2,500, as seems possible to him though the evidence is scanty,[118] would then have possessed 235 slaves for each citizen—six times as many as the wealthy father of Demosthenes owned. There would have had to be scores of men in Aegina who owned as many slaves as Nicias. The same arguments apply also to Corinth's supposed 460,000 slaves. Besides, as he observes, with only approximately as many slaves as Athenaeus records, she could have manned the ninety triremes against Corcyra, but instead she hired 18,000 men from outside.[119] Sixty thousand slaves would have been enough to warrant the term χοινικομέτραι so often applied to the Corinthians.

After this, Beloch proceeds to question the number of 400,000 slaves given for Athens, although he felt, as he wrote later in reply to Seeck,[120] that he was only "breaking through an open door."[121] Unfortunately, however, in 1886 he started the argument at the point at which Hume did in 1752, by taking the numbers in Demetrius' census to refer only to adult male slaves on the grounds that the two preceding numbers referred only to adult males, citizens and metics. This, then, would imply a grand total, of 1,000,000 slaves, or otherwise there would be, in his own words (p. 88), "weder Sinn noch Verstand" in the whole census. This was clearly an error on Beloch's part, and subsequent critics have not failed to point it out, being also inconsistent with his observation (p. 98) upon the number of slaves recorded by Hyperides.

This remark, however, which was, after all, something of an *obiter dictum*, makes no practical difference in the results of his contention, for Beloch (p. 88) grants for the sake of argument that

---

[118]Beloch cites as throwing some light on the question of Aegina's population (*op. cit.*, 122, 3): Herod., VIII, 46; Thucyd., I, 105, 108; Herod., IX, 28; Thucyd., IV, 56, 57. See also his discussion *Griechische Geschichte*, III, 1 (1922), 277, 8, where he estimates Aegina's free population as 2,000—3,000 in the fifth century and still smaller in the fourth.

[119]Thucyd., I, 31, 35.

[120]Seeck, "Die Statistik in der Alten Geschichte," *Jahrb. für Nat-ök.* (1897), 162 ff.

[121]Beloch, "Zur Bevölkerungsgeschichte," *Jahrb. für Nat-ök.* (1897), 324.

the number 400,000 meant all the slaves, and then proceeds to show
that even that number can be shown to be impossible. First, the
valuation of all property in Attica, except that owned by the state
or the gods, was, in the first half of the fourth century b. c., according to three reliable statements from antiquity,[122] from 5,750 to
6,000 talents. Now 400,000 slaves at the very low average value of
1 mina each[123] would alone represent 6,000 talents. Boeckh's hypothesis that the 6,000 talents represented only a portion of a total
30,000 or 40,000 talents, that is, one-fifth of the property of the
first class and a correspondingly smaller proportion of the next
three lower classes, had already been amply refuted by Beloch.[124]
Grote,[125] moreover, had previously shown that the passage from
Aristophanes used by Boeckh (I, 577, 3rd ed.) as important evidence for the existence of at least 20,000 talents of taxable
property, referred to some sort of indirect tax, certainly not a
direct property tax of two and a half percent.

The words of the passage,[126] as Grote says, are far from
describing a direct property assessment in Athens for they hint
at a novel scheme, winning great popularity at first, and thought
likely to raise an enormous sum at one blow but later proving
to be mere empty boasting.

Even if it were not for the facts of the property valuation, we
must consider seriously, continues Beloch (p. 89), what a population of 500,000, such as Boeckh pictured it, implies for Attica.
To feed these would have required, in addition to the importation
of large quantities of grain from abroad, that, according to
Boeckh's computation, one-half of Attica be sown to grain and
2,800,000 medimni raised each year (see Chapter III below). At

[122] a. Polybius, II, 62, 6, (378/7 b. c.)
     b. Demosth., XIV, 19, (354/3 b. c.)
     c. Philochorus, fr. 151 Müller (Harpocration). *V. supra*, 21, note 65.

[123] See Busolt (*op. cit.*, 200) for references in Greek authors to prices of slaves.

[124] "Das Volksvermögen von Attika," *Hermes* 20, (1885), 237 ff. See also J.
Lipsius, Die Attische Steuerverfassung und das Attische Volksvermögen, *Rhein.
Mus. für Philol.* 71 (1916), 161-86.

[125] *History of Greece*, Vol. IX, Chap. 75, 206 ff. (London, 1869).

[126] *Ecclesiaz.*, 823 ff:

       τὸ δ' ἐναγχος οὐχ ἅπαντες ἡμεῖς ὤμνυμεν
       τάλαντ' ἔσεσθαι πεντακόσια τῇ πόλει
       τῆς τεσσαρακοστῆς, ἣν ἐπόρισ' Εὐριπίδης;
       κεὐθὺς κατεχρύσου πᾶς ἀνὴρ Εὐριπίδην, κτλ.

that rate more fertile regions, such as Bœotia, with as much arable land, would have produced at least the same amount, to say nothing of Thessaly, Elis, and Messenia. With their scantier population these states could have exported large quantities of grain, and Greece would have supplied half the world, instead of importing grain as she did from Pontus, Egypt, and elsewhere.

Still another reason makes such a large number of slaves seem improbable to Beloch. At the end of the fourth century B.C. Athens, he reminds us (p. 92), had 12,000 citizens who possessed less than 2,000 drachmas and only 9,000 who had more.[127] These 12,000 then did not have enough to live on,[128] and they must, therefore, have had to work and could have owned slaves in very limited numbers, if at all. The 9,000 probably owned slaves. These with heiresses, widows, corporations, and so forth, Beloch thinks may have formed a total of 15,000 masters for the supposed 400,000 slaves. But this would give an average of about twenty-seven slaves apiece, a deduction which it seems to him (p. 93) is not confirmed by the literary evidence. Finally, the remarks of Thucydides about Chios and about the flight of 20,000 slaves to Decelea, as well as the fact that Xenophon, in his proposition to buy 10,000, felt it necessary to meet the objection that perhaps the mines could not employ so many, militate against the possibility of a proportion of four slaves to one free person.

Beloch next suggests how the mistake might have occurred in the account of Athenaeus. His explanation is (p. 95): "If we recall that the same mark M can express 40 and 10,000, the origin of the error is at once clear. In his source Athenaeus found the numbers M·F and M·Z, overlooked the periods and read 46 and 47 instead of 60,000 and 70,000. The context showed that tens of thousands of slaves were under discussion; what was more natural than to write μυριάδες after the numbers? In the statement taken from Ctesicles in regard to the slaves at Athens, Athenaeus apparently found only the mark for 10,000 (M), while the number of tens of thousands had disappeared, so that the error

---

[127]Diod., XVIII, 18; Plut., *Phoc.*, 28. *V. infra*, 60, note 85, for his later view on this evidence from Diodorus.

[128]Two thousand drachmas at that time would yield an income of 240 drachmas when 360 drachmas were considered necessary for a working man's family (Busolt, *op. cit.*, 203 and Billeter, *Geschichte des Zinsfusses* (Leipzig 1898), 10 ff.).

is still plainer here." There naturally remains, also, so Beloch thinks, the possibility that Ctesicles mentioned τετρακισμύριοι δοῦλοι and that Athenaeus copied it as τετταράκοντα μυριάδες.[129] In fact, Beloch continues, 40,000 adult male slaves for Demetrius' time is not at all improbable. Attica would then have had, on the whole, a slave population of perhaps 100,000 in 309 B. C., because adult men, in his opinion, must have been proportionally more numerous among slaves than among citizens and metics. This hypothesis is somewhat weakened because the 40,000 for Athens given by the census are in Beloch's opinion to be regarded as male slaves only and because, in the case of Aegina, it does not explain why a Scholiast to Pindar[130] should also have recorded 470,000 slaves.

In a new estimate of the exact number of slaves, Beloch finds satisfactory data for only a general picture (pp. 96 ff.). The inscriptional evidence of 329/8 B. c. (p. 91) shows that 400,000 medimni of grain, principally barley, were raised that year in Attica. This, with the importation of 800,000 medimni of wheat mentioned by Demosthenes (XX, 32) about 354 B. c., would provide food for 175,000, reckoning an average per capita consumption of six medimni of wheat or seven of barley, with due allowance for sowing (p. 96 f.). If the figures of the importation are correct, and the harvest of 329/8 a normal one, Beloch believes that an estimate of 100,000 free population and 75,000 slaves for the middle of the fourth century is not far from the truth. Xenophon's statement (*Vectigal.*, IV, 25) that the slave tax before Decelea amounted to more than it did seventy-five years later, coupled with the fact that according to Thucydides (VII, 27) Chios had more slaves than Athens, would lead one to infer, Beloch says (p. 97), a slave population of 100,000 for Athens in 431 B. c. By 378/7 this may have decreased to 60,000 due to

[129]See Ciccotti (*Del Numero*, etc., 658, 661) for an adverse but sane criticism of these hypotheses; *cf.* also Letronne (*op. cit.*, 173 ff.) who believes Athenaeus untrustworthy in view of other exaggerations (Letronne quotes several) and, therefore, that there is no need to verify or emend the passage, but to have recourse to Attic authors who furnish the strongest arguments against so prodigious a number of slaves for Attica. I agree with Letronne.

[130]*Olymp.*, VIII, 30. This may, however, derive directly from Athenaeus or from a source intermediate between him and Ctesicles, in which the error was first made.

the vicissitudes experienced by the city. The property valuation of 5,750 talents would imply a number no larger than that. During the last half of the fourth century, with the increase in material prosperity, the number of slaves, in his opinion, may have risen from 75,000 in 350 B. C. to 100,000 in Alexander's time (p. 98).[131] Hyperides' mention of 150,000 slaves in 338 B. C. Beloch thinks too uncertain a passage to be used as statistical evidence. His emendation, only half-heartedly suggested, that μυριάδας πλέον (sic) ἢ δεκαπέντε be changed to μυριάδας πλέον δ' ἢ ε' has found little favor.[132] If any emendation is to be accepted, the one suggested by Sauppe, and approved by Meyer,[133] may be nearer the truth, i. e., that the imperfect manuscript should be corrected to (μυριάδας) πλείους ἢ δεκαπέντε, πρῶτον μὲν δούλους τοὺς ἐκ τῶν ἔργων, κτλ. The passage would thus merely speak of 150,000 fighting men, the whole number which Hyperides hoped to be able to levy through the arming of the slaves, debtors, and others excluded from the citizen-lists, including the metics. With this interpretation, the fragment would lose all value as a statistical statement about slaves.

In a series of valuable discussions, Meyer,[134] after showing that the number of slaves could not have been as large as sometimes imagined, insists on the basis of the evidence, that, due to the impecunious condition of a large number of citizens, there necessarily existed much manual labor on the part of free men. He is of the opinion that not every citizen or even half of them owned slaves, that Thetes, as well as Zeugites like Socrates, probably owned none, but that the majority of Zeugites may have had one. An admissible maximum, in his opinion, would be 150,000.[135] Since his conclusions agree in general with those of Beloch, it is not necessary to discuss them in detail.

---

[131]See also his remarks, Gr. Gesch., III, I, (1922), 273.

[132]Ciccotti (Del Numero, etc., 658) thinks that this emendation is of little value because the phrase "more than 150,000" is indefinite enough, but that the correction to "four or five tens of thousands" would leave entirely too many thousands to be supplied. V. supra, p. 21.

[133]Forsch. zur alten Gesch., II, 189.

[134]Die Sklaverei im Altertume (1898, 1910), 175 ff.; Die Bevölkerung des Altertums (1891), 444 ff.; Forschungen zur alten Geschichte (1899), II, 185 ff.

[135]Forsch. z. alt. Gesch., II, 188. Geschichte des Altertums, IV, 56.

In an essay,[136] "Del Numero degli Schiavi nell'Attica," Ciccotti very sanely reviews the progress made thus far in the question, and with good reason raises the query, "Really, how far have we progressed since Hume?" Except for contending that the statement of Hyperides is to be accepted as meaning that Attica at the time of that orator had 150,000 slaves, he makes no attempt to estimate the number himself. The other more general statement from Thucydides about Chios merely indicates, in his opinion, that Chios, with one-third the area of Attica, had more slaves than the latter in the fifth century. The institution of slavery, he says, cannot have been very highly developed in Attica, if so small a district as Chios possessed more slaves.[137] As for the numbers recorded in Athenaeus, Ciccotti, like Niebuhr,[138] sees no reason why any thinking man should longer believe them, in view of the objections that have been raised. But he believes that in the efforts to make a new estimate of the number there has been too much guess-work. In unsparing terms, he denounces the favorite method of calculating the numbers of the population by the amount of grain consumed. The discovery of the record of the sacred tribute of grain at Eleusis has given the most categorical refutation to such calculations, and, he adds, it is now to be hoped that the vicious circle is at last broken whereby two unknowns, the amount of grain available and the average consumption, are invoked to find the third unknown, the number of people. Instead of trying to discover the exact number, in his opinion, it is more important to study the population itself in all its various aspects, thereby deducing the real causes for a decrease or increase in the number of slaves.

By the use of these so-called "demographical" data, Ciccotti in his book, *Il Tramonto della Schiavitu,* defends the thesis that slave labor in the fourth century, far from increasing, suffered a notable decrease because of the general economic conditions. By an analysis of political conditions, the state of agriculture, industry, and commerce, the financial condition of the average Athenian citizen which made it necessary for a large majority to work in order to live, and a comparison of the cost of slave and free labor,

---

[136]*Rendiconti del Istituto Lombardo,* 30 (1897), 655-73.
[137]But compare Wallon's treatment of this evidence (*v. infra,* 25 ff.).
[138]*Röm. Geschichte* (1873), II, 71.

he reaches the conclusion that in the fourth century b. c. the use of slavery was noticeably declining in favor of contract labor which employed preferably free workers.[139] Nor, as he points out, could the small amount received from the state for jury duty, attendance at festivals, or the theatre ever have totalled enough to take the proletariat from work, and encourage a life of ease. It could not have amounted on the average, at the very highest figure, to an assured revenue of more than three obols a day, and that, according to Aristophanes,[140] represented hardly the daily pay of one of the lowest classes of workmen. It would have bought only one-sixth medimnus of wheat at the lowest price. Many men no doubt preferred to work than try to live on such donations. The gradual increase of distributions, far from being a means of turning workmen from their trade, is a proof, he thinks, that the professional labor of great numbers rendered necessary the payment of an indemnity intended to compensate them for the time taken from their professional work[141] by the care of affairs of state, and to prevent them from deserting public assemblies.

Since 1900, several studies of the economic life of Athens have been devoted to a consideration of conditions of labor, and a few separate articles have been published. Francotte,[142] who quotes the views of Hume and Beloch favorably, would suggest, although with considerable hesitation, 75,000 to 100,000 as a possible number for the slaves in Attica. Guiraud in three discussions between 1893 and 1905 has expressed gradually changing views. In the earliest,[143] he regards the number left by Athenaeus as not improbable and well-supported by the Hyperides' fragment, which he interprets as meaning a levy of 150,000 slaves of military age, which would imply a total of at least 400,000. The next,[144] a more

---

[139]The most important evidence cited is: Xen., *Mem.*, II, 7-10 (a picture of conditions in Athens at the end of the Peloponnesian War). *I. G.*, I, 324; *cf.* 321, 325; II, 834 b, c; IV, 2, 834 b (accounts of the building of the Erectheum and the shrine at Eleusis, giving the number of workers and the different classes to which they belonged).

[140]*Ecclesiaz.*, 310.

[141]Xen., *Mem.*, III, 7, 6; Xenophon represents Socrates as picturing the assembly composed of smiths, carpenters, farmers, tradespeople, etc.

[142]*L'Industrie dans la Grèce Ancienne* (1900), I, 161 ff.

[143]*La Propriété Foncière* (1893), 157 ff.

[144]*La Main d'Oeuvre Industrielle dans l'ancienne Grèce*, (1900), 103, 4 ff.

thorough treatment of labor problems, merely suggests that the Hyperides' fragment shows that the total was more than 150,000 and that the general impression is that the slaves were more numerous in Greece than the free. But in 1905[145] he states positively that the numbers of Athenaeus are evidently false, yet without adducing any concrete proof of his belief, he thinks that 100,000 is too small a number to substitute arbitrarily when we reflect that the majority of Athenian families were served by slaves, that certain ones possessed more than fifty, and that texts worthy of credence mention masters who had from 600 to 1,000. (But *cf.* 67 *infra* and note.)

To Cavaignac,[146] the estimates of 100,000 for the fifth century and 150,000 for the fourth seem to be reasonable, but Gernet,[147] echoing the arguments of Boeckh which have been already cited, and adding no new proof, thinks that there are not yet enough reasons for calling Athenaeus' number wrong "because, even supposing that 5000 of the poorest did or did not have slaves, the total would not be changed." Zaborowski[148] summarily dismisses the question by the apparently original observation, "without doubt in these exaggerated figures should be included metics."

Zimmern,[149] in his well elaborated discussion of chattel and apprentice slavery, is more interested in analyzing the varieties of slavery in Greece than in fixing the numbers. Following Cairnes'[150] analysis he reaches the conclusion that the conditions characteristic of a slave state by no means existed in Attica. Cairnes' typical slave state is a community of slaves, idlers, and slave-drivers too savage to enjoy the refinements of civilization and if it were not too savage, too poor, to pay for them. There is nothing here, Zimmern says, to remind us of the communities which, untaught and unaided, by sheer exercise of enterprise and insight created the civilization of the Western World. If we adopt the familiar theory that the Greek city state was a slave state, he continues, then we must admit that nearly every Greek was a

---

[145] *Études Économiques*, 129 f.

[146] *Études sur l'Histoire Financière d'Athènes au Ve Siècle*, (1908), 172 ff.

[147] *L'Approvisionnement d'Athènes en Blé* (1909), 273 ff.

[148] "Ancient Greece and its Slave Population," *Annual Report of Smithsonian Institute*, (1912), 597 ff.

[149] "Was Greek Civilization Based on Slave Labor?" *Soc. Rev.*, (1909), 176 ff.

[150] *The Slave Power, its Character, Career, and Probable Design* (1862), 140 ff.

slave-owner and shared a supposedly characteristic Greek aversion to manual labor. "But even if we had no Greek literature, the remains of Greek architecture alone would suffice to destroy the fable that the Greeks were a race of impractical contemplative aesthetes who kept a tribe of tame drudges to minister to their material needs. Instead of all being mere chattel slaves, many were in a sort of apprentice slavery; instead of being the mere possession of a master, the slave, considered as an individual, was given some motive for working: perhaps a chance to marry, to buy his freedom, or to live away from his master." As for competition between free and slave labor, a few occupations, he thinks, may have been reserved for each, but in many the freeman and the slave worked side by side. Plutarch (*Pericles,* 12) shows that building was a free man's industry, and the big state buildings were undertaken partly in order to give citizens employment. An inscription (*I. G.,* I, 324), Zimmern reminds us, gives the information that at the building of the Erectheum in 408 B. C., twenty-seven citizens, forty metics, and fifteen slaves were working together. Inscriptions from the building of the sanctuary at Eleusis in 329/8 and 319/8 (*I. G.,* II, 834, b, c.; IV², 834b) show a total of thirty-six citizens, thirty-nine metics, and two slaves, together with fifty-seven other names too indefinite to be put in any category. Here are, as he says, at least three definite instances where free men and slaves were working at the same trade. In the case of the Erectheum, in squads of four to six people directed by a foreman, they were busied in fluting columns, and all, including the foreman, received the same pay.

Oldfather, in an article "Slavery as an Economic Institution,"[151] argues that from definite literary evidence not more than half of the total population of Athens could have afforded to own slaves. As to the common misconception that in Athens there was a general aversion to manual labor, of course that might be true among the aristocracy and philosophers, but that signifies very little because the Greeks habitually expressed quite openly what moderns of the same social class feel, no doubt, quite as strongly but hesitate to express. The celebrated funeral oration of Pericles contains one significant sentence apropos of the common man,

---

[151] *The Progressive Journal of Education* (1910), 116 ff.

"Disgrace consists not in confessing one's poverty but in not working so as to escape it."[152] Many men, in his opinion, seemed not
ashamed of their callings, since bakers, carpenters, potters, smiths,
and masons had inscribed their names and callings as early as the
sixth century on their tombstones. Furthermore, he reminds us,
a law was passed at Athens against idlers, by which every man
had to profess some occupation.[153] Another law freed from the
obligation to support his aged father a son who had not been
taught a trade.[154] In Athens, also, it was a legally recognized form
of slander,[155] punishable by the courts, to reproach a man or
woman with his calling. In a recent book, *Greek Life and
Thought* (New York), 1923), Van Hook has expressed much the
same views (p. 95). "Now the old-fashioned assumption that the
Athenians found abundant leisure and opportunity for the *real life*
(*i. e.*, art, literature, politics, and philosophy) only because slaves
and women did everything for them and the state treasury liber-
ally supported them in *dolce far niente* is ridiculous. One thing is
certain from all we know of the Athenians: they were not indolent;
they were energetic in mind and body. Certainly in any State the
wealthy are but a minority of the total population and even upon
these rests the duty to manage their property and care for investments." After a discussion of the social and economic conditions of
the latter half of the fifth century and the causes for the current mis-
conceptions regarding them, he reaches the conclusion (pp. 106-7):
"Finally the almost universal assumption that Athenian achieve-
ments were possible *only through slavery,* and that slavery was
the *dominant* factor in Athenian economic life, is a gross exaggeration. On the contrary, the slaves were in the minority in the
total population in the latter half of the fifth century B. C. and
the prosperity and greatness of the city-state was due not to the
exploitation of slave labor, but to the industry, the initiative, and
the efficiency of citizen and metic, in whose hands the political,

[152]Thucyd., II, 40.
[153]Plutarch, *Solon*, 22. *Cf. Corpus Iuris Attici*, 192-96.
[154]Plutarch, *Solon*, 22.
[155]Demosth., LVII, 30, 31.

the intellectual, the artistic, and the commercial fortunes rested."[156] He accepts 300,000 to 400,000 as an estimate of the total population in Athens and Attica at about the year 431 B. C., and in his opinion (p. 80) these consisted of: adult male citizens, between 40,000 and 55,000, and with their wives and children, far above 100,000; resident aliens or metics, 14,000 to 24,000, with their families perhaps 50,000; slaves, *adult males*, perhaps 50,000. In a previous article[157] Van Hook had emphasized the fact that some of the gravest mistakes in the question have been caused by a disregard of the chronological factor, for Athens in the second half of the fifth century in political, social, and economic conditions was by no means the Athens of the sixth and fourth centuries. The second grave error, in his opinion, arises from taking the ideal and aristocratic conceptions of Plato and Aristotle literally as reflecting actual conditions.

In two other recent volumes, it is significant to note that there is no longer any discussion of the possibility of 400,000 slaves for Attica. That number, it is now generally agreed, is absurd. Glotz[158] briefly classifies the slave population as Wallon did, but corrects his predecessor by showing that agriculture employed relatively few slaves. In Busolt's[159] recent *Griechische Staatskunde* there is no detailed discussion of the problem, but the volume contains a mass of critically sifted and admirably classified information about the political, social, and economic life of the ancient Greeks, a knowledge of which is essential to such a study as this.

[156]See also the remarks of Ferguson (*Greek Imperialism* 61, 63, and 64) pertinent to this question: "The demands put upon the time of Athenian citizens by the state were enormous, but not such as to cripple economic production. A comparison with modern conditions will make this clear. A little less frequently than once a week the ecclesia met, but the attendance was less than one-tenth of those qualified. That represents a suspension of work roughly equivalent to our Saturday afternoons and legal holidays. A little oftener than once a week a contest or other public festival occurred, and to these there was, it seems, a pretty general resort. They correspond to our Fair Days and Sundays. Preparation for the contests was perhaps not more destructive of money-earning time than our collegiate and university courses. . . . Athens regularly employed a committee of ten to do one man's work with the result that all of them were free to give nine-tenths of their time to private business."

[157]"Was Athens in the Age of Pericles Aristocratic?" *Classical Journal*, 14, (1918-19), 472 ff.

[158]*Le Travail dans la Grèce Ancienne* (1920), 236 ff.

[159]Müller's *Handbuch*, etc., IV, 1, 1 (1920, 3rd ed.).

It has, I trust, been made sufficiently clear from the preceding review of the critical studies of the past century and a half that the statistical method of inquiry alone has not yet yielded satisfactory results, for the evidence is too scanty and furthermore will admit varying interpretations. On the other hand, the separate passages bearing on the subject from the literature of the two centuries may severally be vague, or subject to more than one interpretation, but taken as a whole their cumulative effect is considerable, if it should appear that no single passage requires an assumption which is inconsistent with a hypothesis that will adequately explain them all. True it is, that the writers, being for the most part members of the more favored classes of society, have a tendency to leave a clearer picture of men like Nicias, Xenophon, Pasion, or Demosthenes, than of any typical three-obol-a-day working man. But there is every reason to believe that whatever statements have been left us, inadvertently, by the Attic authors regarding the rank and file of the populace are a much more valuable basis for authoritative conclusions than those derived, for example, from hypothetical measures of barley, raised from a hypothetical amount of seed on a hypothetical amount of land divided among people with hypothetically increasing or decreasing appetites. Hume[160] was right when he wrote: "Many grounds of calculation proceeded on by celebrated writers are little better than those of Emperor Heliogabalus when he formed an estimate of the immense greatness of Rome from the ten thousand pounds of cobwebs he had found in the city."[161]

[160]*Op. cit.*, 414.
[161]Aelii Lamprid., *Vita Heliogab.*, 26.

CHAPTER II

THE NUMBER OF SLAVES IN DOMESTIC SERVICE[1]

Numerous references in the Attic authors show that it was customary for many Athenian families to use slaves about the house. When the metic Callias was brought to court on a μήνυσις presented by his slaves, an orator said to the jury in his defense: "In my opinion this case does not concern merely these individuals but everyone in the city for you all have slaves (θεράποντες)."[1a] Demosthenes likewise represented Apollodorus as saying to the jury: "I will tell you what is the best way to comprehend the magnitude of my wrongs. You must each of you consider what servant you left at home, and then imagine that you have suffered from him the same treatment which I have suffered from this man. No matter if his name is Syrus or Manes or some other, and this man's name is Phormio. The thing is the same—they are slaves, and this man was a slave; you are masters, and I was a master."[2] From Aristotle comes the statement that "a complete household consists of slaves and freemen."[3]

The families fortunate enough to have slaves kept them busy in divers ways. Slaves acted as faithful nurses to the children,[4] as paedagogi;[5] they accompanied their mistress to the festival,[6] and their master out to the farm in the early morning, or carried his luggage on longer trips.[7] They ran errands interminably over to the neighbors for a bronze pitcher or for extra bedding and cups for guests, to the bank for money, or to the market for provisions.[8] In the house they tended the door, helped to prepare the meals, and to make some of the clothes, kept written accounts, and

[1]As Wallon has previously done, I shall now classify the slaves according to their occupations and shall try to estimate the probable number of each group.

[1a]Lysias, V, 5.

[2]XLV, 86 (Kennedy's transl.).

Polit., I, 2, 1. οἰκία δὲ τέλειος ἐκ δούλων καὶ ἐλευθέρων.

[4]Demosth., XLVII, 55; Aristoph., *Thesmoph.*, 608; Menander, *Samia*, 22.

[5]Xen., *Pol. Laced.*, II, 1; Theophrast., *Charact.*, IX, 15.

[6]Aristoph., *Thesmoph.*, 277, 293.

[7]Antiphon, II, 1, 9; Xen., *Oec.*, XI, 15; *Mem.*, II, 13, 6. Aristoph., *Ranae* (beginning).

[8]Lysias, I, 14; Demosth., XLVII, 52; XLIX, 22; Theophrast., *Charact.*,XVIII, 2; XXIII, 2; Menander, *Periceir.*, 34.

assisted in religious ceremonies, besides the usual duties of a valet
and lady's maid.[9] In court they were used as important witnesses
for or against their master.[10] Not only were slaves a customary
part of the household but they were also a very valued part of it.
If they were ill, doctors were hastily summoned; in their master's
will they were sometimes rewarded for faithful services, and
Aristotle even counselled that some sort of recreation be provided
for them.[11] A slave who had been freed was welcomed back in
some homes to spend an impoverished old age,[12] and a master
would undertake a long journey and incur considerable expense
to recover a runaway slave.[13]

In this system of domestic servitude, however, there are several
significant features. First, slaves appear to be used mainly for
necessary work, not for purposes of ostentation, in fact any arro-
gant display of servants is severely frowned upon.[14] Additional

[9]Xen., *Oec.*, VII, 6; X, 10; Demosth., XXIX, 11; XXXIII, 18; Aristoph.,
Acharn., 249; Lycurg., *c. Leocr.*, 55; Theophrast., *Charact.*, XXII, 10.

[10]Andocides, I, 12; Demosth., LII, 22; Lycurg., *c. Leocr.*, 30; Lysias, V, 3; 4.

[11]Xen., *Mem.*, II, 4, 3; Plato, *Leg.*, IV, 10; Diog. Laert., V, 4, 74; Aristot., *Oec.*,
I, 5, 20.

[12]Demosth., XLVII, 55.

[13]Xen., *Mem.*, II, 10, 2; Demosth., LIII, 6.

[14]Demosthenes charges against Meïdias that instead of rendering services to the
state (XXI, 158): "He . . . built a house at Eleusis so large as to darken all in
the place; and he carries his wife to the mysteries, or anywhere else that she likes,
with his white pair from Sicyon; and he himself pushes through the market place
with three or four attendants . . ." (Kennedy's transl.), and again (XXXVI, 45)
he prejudices the jury against Apollodorus by saying: ". . . and you take three
foot boys about you, and live so indecently that even people meeting you in the
streets perceive it" (Kennedy's transl.). The Athenians seem to have been singu-
larly moderate in the use of slaves as escorts through town or on longer journeys.
The permissible number for a respectable and wealthy man or woman to employ
on ordinary occasions for such purposes was only one. A few of the many references in literature to this are: Antiphon, II, 1, 9; Lycurg., *c. Leocr.*, 55; Theophrast., *Charact.*, XXII, 10; XXX, 7. The poorer people naturally had none.
Aristophanes (*Ecclesiaz.*, 593) represents the women as claiming that when they
get the vote they will correct this inequality, μηδ᾽ ἀνδραπόδοις τὸν μὲν χρῆσθαι πολ-
λοῖς τὸν δ᾽ οὐδ᾽ ἀκολούθῳ. That Diogiton (Lysias, XXXII, 16) was accused of
turning his brother's children out of doors penniless, without extra clothes, *or an
attendant*, does not seem to me to be proof, though others have used it as such
(*cf.* Rogers' note to Aristophanes, *Ecclesiaz.*, 593) that it was a sign of extreme
destitution not to have a slave attendant. The fact was that the father of these
children had left them a fortune of over eight talents (28), so it would be a very
heartless guardian indeed, who would not allow heirs of such wealth even one servant.

ones were usually hired from the market to assist on any special occasion requiring more work than usual.[15] There is no indication that the Athenians accepted the suggestion of the philosopher, Democritus,[16] to use slaves as parts of the body were used, one for each purpose. The records of literature would tend to show rather, that more often one slave was used for every purpose as in the case of the poor Athenian[17] with social aspirations who summoned his one servant by a different name each time to impress his guests with his staff of helpers. Moreover, not all the work connected with the food and clothing of the household was performed by slaves at home.[18] It is not so surprising to find that the finest wraps were bought ready made, but it is somewhat strange to learn that the coarse garments worn by laborers were frequently purchased outside the house. More than half of the citizens of Megara were employed in the manufacture of this staple article, the ἐξωμίς;[19] Menon, the mantua-maker, and Collytus, manufacturer of cloaks, had a prosperous business even in the years directly after the Peloponnesian War. As for the food bought outside, we may safely conclude that baker's bread was no unfamiliar article in the homes of the fourth century before Christ. Cyrebus, so Xenophon states, lived in the lap of luxury from the proceeds of his bread-shop.[20] In families, too, even where there was considerable wealth, the wife and the daughters knew from actual practice how to perform efficiently the various duties of spinning, baking, and the like.[21]

[15]Theophrast., *Charact.*, XXII, 4.

[16]Stob., LXII, 45. This chance remark has often been cited to support the view of a noteworthy "gaspillage" in employing servants in the home. Wallon, *op. cit.*, 236; Guiraud, *La Main d'Oeuvre*, etc., 124; Beauchet in *Daremberg-Saglio*, IV, 1271; Glotz, *op. cit.*, 242.

Plato's statement (*Resp.*, IX, 578), which others quote on this point, that a rich man sometimes owned fifty slaves, does not give any information as to how many a rich man employed in his home. The number merely indicates all those in his possession for any purpose. *Cf.*, Wallon, *op. cit.*, 236; Richter, *op. cit.*, 95.

[17]Athen., VI, 230 c.

[18]Xen., *Cyropaed.*, VIII, 2, 5.

[19]Xen., *Mem.*, II, 7, 6; Aristoph., *Pax*, 1002.

[20]Xen., *Mem.*, II, 7, 7; *cf.*, Aristoph., *Vesp.*, 1388-91; *Ranae*, 857; *Frag.*, 313 (Hall & Geldart).

[21]Xen., *Pol. Laced.*, I, 3; *Oec.*, VII, 6; *Mem.*, II, 7, 8; Aristoph., *Lysistr.*, 15-20.

A second important fact to consider is that to buy slaves and maintain them in the home required money from which investment there was little or no cash return, as was not the case when slaves were let out for hire. The initial cost of slaves varied considerably, of course, but a little less than two minas may be taken as a fair average.[22] As for feeding and clothing them, we have the information that it cost the state about 225 drachmas apiece, yearly, or not quite two-thirds of a drachma per day to provide maintenance for its seventeen slave workmen in 329/8 B. C.[23] The cost to a private family would not, of course, be as much, but yet it must have been of some consequence.[24] It would be reasonable, then, to suppose that many families were too poor to afford the

[22]The average price of the seven sold, when the property of several implicated in the mutilation of the Hermae was confiscated, was about one and four-fifths minas. *I. G.*, I, 274, 275, 277; IV, 1, 274. Xenophon (*Mem.*, II, 5, 2) says that a slave might cost anywhere from one-half a mina to ten. Demosthenes (LIII, 1) speaks of two farm slaves valued together at two and one-half minas, but gives the price elsewhere (XLI, 8) as two minas for one.

[23]*I. G.*, II, 2, 834b; *I. G.*, IV, 2, 834b. *Cf.* Wazynski, *De Servis Atheniensium Publicis*, 47; and Glotz, *Le Travail dans la Grèce Ancienne*, 256.

[24]Some idea of the cost of maintenance per person may be gained from Lysias (XXXII, 28). There the speaker declares that an average of three drachmas a day for the maintenance of two boys, one girl, a male, and a female slave, is a larger sum than anyone in the city ever paid. There would be definite record of the cost of board of fifteen slaves for ten years if Kennedy's translation of a passage from Demosthenes could be substantiated. Kennedy's version (vol. IV, 102) is: "From the seventy-seven minas, proceeds of the manufactory, I must deduct the maintenance of the men on whom (as I admit) Therippides spent seven minas a year. In ten years the maintenance comes to seventy minas, leaving a balance upon this account in my favor of seven minas;" but the orator's words (XXVII, 36) do not seem to warrant such a translation: τὴν μὲν τοίνυν τροφὴν ἀπὸ τῶν ἑβδομήκοντα μνῶν καὶ ἑπτὰ λογιστέον, τῶν ἀπὸ τοῦ ἐργαστηρίου γενομένων. Θηριππίδης γὰρ ἑπτὰ μνᾶς ἐδίδου καθ' ἕκαστον τὸν ἐνιαυτὸν εἰς ταῦτα, καὶ ἡμεῖς τοῦτο λαβεῖν ὁμολογοῦμεν. ὥσθ' ἑβδομήκοντα μνῶν ἐν τοῖς δέκ' ἔτεσι τροφὴν τούτων ἡμῖν ἀνηλωκότων, τὸ περιὸν τὰς ἑπτακοσίας προστίθημ' αὐτοῖς. It is difficult to see how τροφὴν can be understood as referring to that of the slaves in view of the words: ἡμεῖς τοῦτο λαβεῖν ὁμολογοῦμεν and again τροφὴν ἡμῖν ἀνηλωκότων. In averaging the net income of the factory as eleven minas it is more likely that the maintenance of the slaves was deducted before this with the rest of the expenses. The contents of the oration as a whole would seem to show that Boeckh (*op. cit.*, I, 145, 3rd ed.) and Schaefer (*Demosthenes und seine Zeit*, I, 279, 2nd ed.) are correct in interpreting the passage to mean that out of the proceeds of the factory seven minas were paid yearly toward the maintenance of Demosthenes, his sister, and his mother.

luxury of slave assistance in the home.[25] Xenophon,[26] in fact, remarks, "If a citizen has the means he will employ slaves that he may have assistants in his work." Aristophanes[27] corroborates this with the statement that some use many slaves but others not even one. Aristotle,[28] too, definitely states, "the poor, not having any slaves, must employ both their women and children as servants."

Consequently, the problem of estimating the number of slaves in domestic service resolves itself into something more than describing the interiors of those few wealthy households of which we have rather complete data. It will be necessary to state approximately how many in Athens belonged at different periods during the fifth and fourth centuries before Christ to the rich, the middle, and the poor classes.[29] Then, by illustrations from typical homes of each of these groups, we may be able to infer a possible number of slaves employed in all the households.

I shall discuss first οἱ πλούσιοι, that is, the members of the two wealthiest classes. Some clue to the amount of income required in the fifth century to be counted among the few richest[30] is given by the classification of citizens ascribed by some to Solon, by others to Draco.[31] An income of 500 measures of grain, wine, or oil, at a time when one measure was equivalent to one drachma,[32] was enough to enable one to belong to the privileged group, the Pentacosiomedimni. Whoever had an income of from 300 to 500

---

[25]Aristotle says (*Polit.*, IV, 3, 1): "In the first place we see that all states are made up of families and in the multitude of citizens there must be some rich and some poor, and some in a middle condition. Of the common people, some are husbandmen, and some traders, and some artisans. There are also among the notables differences of wealth and property, for example, in the number of horses which they keep, for they cannot afford to keep them unless they are rich" (Jowett's transl.).

[26]*Mem.*, II, 3, 3.

[27]*Ecclesiaz.*, 593 (*v. supra*, 45, note 14).

[28]*Polit.*, VI, 5, 11.

[29]These are termed by Aristotle (*Polit.*, IV, 11): οἱ μὲν εὔποροι σφόδρα, οἱ δὲ ἄποροι σφόδρα, οἱ δὲ τρίτοι οἱ μέσον τούτων. *Cf.* also Euripides' description of them (*Supplic.*, 238-45).

[30]Aristot., *Polit.*, IV, 3, 12. "Again because the rich are generally few in number, while the poor are many, they appear to be antagonistic" (Jowett's transl.).

[31]Plutarch, *Solon*, 18; Aristot., *Pol. Ath.*, 7.

[32]Plutarch, *Solon*, 23. See also on this point, Busolt, *op. cit.*, 187.

measures a year belonged to the next most wealthy group called
Hippeis, since that was theoretically enough to enable one to keep
a horse. This distinction in classes seems to have been maintained
when the general property requirements of Solon were later translated into terms of money. The person, apparently, with only one
talent of taxable property belonged to the Pentacosiomedimni
group,[33] and those with little more than half that (thirty-six
minas) to the Hippeis.

When we consider that upon these two groups fell the onerous
duty of performing costly liturgies for the state,[34] we understand
why there was a marked tendency in the fourth century, when
prices had soared, to conceal one's wealth rather than by an
extravagant display of it to risk being called upon more often
for patriotic expenditures.[35] This may have acted as a check
against any very large retinue of servants in the house. Orators
frequently seek to discredit an opponent by claiming that he lives
in too large a house, or has been seen with too many attendants.[36]

The average wealth of these two classes, the Pentacosiomedimni
and Hippeis, should not be over-estimated.[37] In the fifth century
there were a few individual fortunes of great size, such as the two
hundred talents of Callias and the one hundred of Nicias, but these
amounts were most exceptional, and Lysias quotes the figures to
show that these fortunes did not last even through the second

---

[33]See Busolt, *op. cit.*, 187; Gilbert, *Griechische Staatsalterthümer* II, 143 ff.
(2nd ed.).

[34]One citizen (Lysias, XXI, 1; 2) boasts that he has expended more than ten
talents in services, which he claims is four times more than the letter of the law
required. Xenophon (*Oec.*, II, 2-7) reports an interesting conversation between
Socrates and Critobulus who is rated as one of the wealthiest of his day. By
enumerating all the expenses contingent upon maintaining such a position in society,
Socrates proves to Critobulus that with all of his 500 minas of property he is no
better off than a poor man with five minas of property. Lysias mentions another man
(XIX, 55; 57; 59) who in the course of a lifetime also expended about ten talents
for the state.

[35]Isocrates, XV, 159; 160: νῦν δ' ὑπὲρ τοῦ μὴ πλουτεῖν ὥσπερ τῶν μεγίστων
ἀδικημάτων ἀπολογίαν δεῖ παρασκευάζεσθαι καὶ σκοπεῖν εἰ μέλλει τις σωθήσεσθαι, κτλ.

[36]Demosth., XXI, 158; XXIII, 206, 207; XXXVI, 45.

[37]Lysias (XIX, 49) calls attention to this common blunder of over-estimating
the wealth of men of old: φαινόμεθα δὴ καὶ τῶν ἀρχαιοπλούτων πολὺ ἐψευσμένοι.

generation.[38] In the fourth century, even though the purchasing power of money was less than in the fifth, a property of ten talents was considered a fortune.[39] Some rather poor men are found listed in the Three Hundred, supposedly a group of the wealthy selected to serve as Trierarchs.[40]

The question is, in these prosperous families where extreme wealth was the exception, how many slaves were regularly employed to carry on the work of the household?[41] The answer cannot be stated exactly; we can only infer the average number from the incidental passages bearing on the subject which will be discussed at this point. If we believe Demosthenes, even prominent

---

[38]XIX, 45 ff. Among these are Ischomachus, supposed to have seventy talents, but leaving his son only ten; Stephanus with more than seventy leaving behind only eleven; Nicias' son leaving fourteen talents; the grandson of Callias leaving but two talents.

[39]Xen., *Oec.*, II, 3 ff. Isaeus, V, 35. Thirteen to sixteen talents are regarded as a large sum (Aristoph., *Plut.*, 193). See Busolt, *op. cit.*, 188 ff.

[40]Demosth., XLII, 22; this man, seeking an exchange of properties with the wealthy Phaenippus, says that his father left him three-fourths of a talent on the income from which it was not easy to live. *V. infra*, 105, note 104.

[41]In selecting typical homes of fifth and fourth century Attica, I should like to call attention here briefly, as it is my intention to present the matter in greater detail soon in a separate article, to the fact that the very wealthy ones described in New Comedy at the close of the fourth century where the plots hinge upon slaves and large sums of money, cannot be regarded as representative of Athenian society in general (but *cf.* Beloch, *Gr. Gesch.*, III, I, (1922) 365, and LeGrand, *Daos* (1910), 81. With due allowance for the fourth and third century decrease in purchasing power of money, the supposed wealth of these families in comedy is extraordinary, as these few concrete instances may suffice to show: In the *Cistellaria* of Plautus the great wealth of the family is indicated (559-61) by:

> Ego te reduco et revoco ad summas ditias
> Ubi tu locere in luculentam familiam
> Unde tibi *talenta magna viginti* pater det *dotis*.

Cf. Trinummus, 1158: spondeo et *mille auri Phillipum dotis; Truculentus*, 845: *sex talenta magna dotis* demam pro ista inscitia; Terence, *Andria*, 952 (dowry of ten talents).

With this should be compared the statement from a fifth century Attic orator (Andocid., IV, 13) who says that Alcibiades received ten talents as a dowry when he married the daughter of Hipponicus [the richest man (II, 130) in Greece], a dowry such as no one of the Greeks had ever received. Demosthenes (XLV, 66) in the fourth century accuses Stephanus of evading public duties though he had a fortune large enough to give his daughter a dowry of one and two-thirds talents. According to the orator (XXV, II, 55) the sister of Demosthenes was bequeathed

citizens in the days of Themistocles lived very simply.[42] That the scale of living later was, on the whole, not extravagant, is indicated in general by the references to domestic expenditures. Demosthenes, whose estate was classed with the largest of his time,[43] says (363 B. c.): "Such being as you have heard, the value of my estate, the third part yielding an income of fifty minas, the guardians though insatiably covetous though resolved not to grant a lease might, out of this income, have maintained us, paid the public taxes, and saved the residue."[44]

Besides these general indications of a simple style of living during the two centuries in question, there is a little more definite evidence in specific cases. Interesting in this connection is the case of a certain Choregus for whom Antiphon pleads (about 412 B. c.). Accused of murder because one of the boys being trained for the festivities of the Thargelia had died at his house from the

two talents as a dowry by her father, one of the wealthiest men of his time (*v. infra*, 97, 98).

In the *Mostellaria* (647, 904 ff.) Plautus represents Simo, the aged Athenian, as greatly pleased that his son purchased a house at as good a bargain as two talents, and saying that he would not accept six talents for it. But prices of houses mentioned by the Attic writers are much lower. The father of Demosthenes, one of the richest men of his day, lived in a house valued at one-half a talent (Demosth., XXVII, 10). Other residences valued from five to fifty minas are mentioned in Lys., XIX, 29; Isaeus, VI, 33; VIII, 35; XI, 42; Lycurg., *c. Leocr.*, 22, 3. The highest price recorded for a private residence seems to be five-sixths of a talent. See also Busolt, *op. cit.*, 199.

Terence (*Heauton.*, 140 ff.) states that all the household effects of Menedemus, including slaves, furniture, house, etc., brought fifteen talents. Now the house (including workshop), slaves, and furniture of Demosthenes' father, considered a wealthy man, were estimated at only two talents (Demosth., XXVII, 10). Everything that Critobulus owned, and he admitted to Socrates that he would be considered very wealthy, was valued at 500 minas (less than nine talents) (Xen., *Oec.*, II, 4).

In the case of the poor or the miserly, the picture seems to be practically the same as in the Attic authors. Euclio and his daughter have one aged slave for a housekeeper (Plautus, *Aulularia*, 39 ff.); in another play one poor maid helps the old women to earn a living by weaving (Terence, *Heauton.*, 292); Geta, the slave, (Terence, *Adelphoe*, 478-82) earns a livelihood for the poor family, and is the sole support of the whole household (647).

[42]XXIII, 206.

[43]*Cf.*, *infra*, 97, 98.

[44]XXVII, 9; 60, 61 (Kennedy's transl.). *Cf.* with this, the passage already quoted (*supra*, 47) from Lysias (XXXII, 28), where three drachmas a day is cited as a preposterous amount to allow for the maintenance of three children and two slaves.

results of a drink of something intended to improve his voice, he emphasizes that the affair took place before the eyes of the entire household.[45] After repeated assertions to this effect, he finally gives a numerical estimate of the members of his house. "For there were more than fifty witnesses of the affair, free men and slaves, adults and boys, who missed nothing that was said or done on the occasion of that distressing incident."[46] Now this was one of the wealthiest households of his tribe, for the man had undertaken to train at his home and entirely at his expense the fifty boys chosen for the dances.[47] Antiphon, too, states elsewhere:[48] αἱ δ' εἰσφοραὶ καὶ χορηγίαι εὐδαιμονίας μὲν ἱκανὸν σημεῖόν ἐστι. On this occasion the Choregus had employed four free men to train the boys and to provide everything for their comfort.[49] At such times one might expect that the force of slaves would be increased, but the speaker includes the fifty boys, the four men, and the slaves in the home in the expression "more than fifty." This is only a rough estimate of the exact number, but it would seem that if the slaves had amounted to twenty-five the expression would have been "more than seventy-five," for the witnesses. I think it would be more natural to assume that the total number of all the persons in the house was between fifty and sixty, and that therefore the slaves were not more than six in number, even in so wealthy a household as this.

In the oration against his guardians, Demosthenes gives the well-known inventory of his father's estate.[50] Two statements here throw some light upon the number of servants in his household. The house,[51] he says, that his father left (in 376 B. C.) was valued

[45]VI, 11 ff.
[46]VI, 22.
[47]See Schneider, *Das Attische Theaterwesen* (1835), 142; also Schol. Aeschin., I, 10: ἐξ ἔθους Ἀθηναῖοι κατὰ φύλας ἵστασαν ν' παίδων χορὸν ἢ ἀνδρῶν, ὥστε γενέσθαι δέκα χορούς, ἐπειδὴ καὶ δέκα φυλαί. διαγωνίζονται δ' ἀλλήλοις διθυράμβῳ, φυλάττοντος τοῦ χορηγοῦντος ἑκάστῳ χωρῷ τὰ ἐπιτήδεια.   For a later system of choosing choregi, see Aristot., *Pol. Ath.*, 56.
[48]*Tetralogia*, I, 3, 8.
[49]VI, 12, 13.
[50]XXVII, 10.
[51]This house seems to have been not only the place of residence for the family but the shop as well, for no record is left in their inventory of another building used by the slave workmen. Bolkestein (*Fabrieken en Fabrikanten in Griekenland*, 14 f.), discusses this and concludes (p. 16): "Naar de werkplaats behoeft men in de boedelbeschrijving van Demosthenes niet meer te zoeken; zij was inbegrepen in het daarbij vermelde huis."

at thirty minas and all the furnishings, including furniture, plate, jewels, clothing, and so forth, were worth altogether one hundred minas.[52] Later he states that Aphobus on entering the house took possession of the jewelry and plate, which were worth fifty minas.[53] This would leave another fifty minas for all the rest of the equipment in the house. Allowing as a maximum amount more than half, that is, thirty minas as the value of the servants, that would mean that in the household of one of the richest men of his day, a man with fourteen talents of property, there were certainly not more than fifteen slaves and probably far fewer than that.[54] Still another statement (35) acts as a check upon the estimate of the value and consequently of the number of these θεράπαιναι whom Demosthenes definitely asserts Aphobus seized. "Observe, the defendant confesses to having received a hundred and eight minas out of my effects." The orator has previously explained (13) that the marriage portion of eighty minas was secured by seizing fifty minas' worth of jewelry and plate, and by appropriating thirty minas from the proceeds of the work-shop, which would leave twenty-eight minas as the value of the household slaves whom he seized.[55]

Isaeus[56] gives more definite information (about 375 B. C.) in the case of Ciron's estate, and this is especially valuable because there were probably many in the two upper classes with property of just such a nature and value as his: a farm in Phlya valued at a talent, two houses in town, one of which was rented and valued at

[52]Although household slaves are not specifically mentioned in the inventory, as is often the case in such lists given by the orators, it is certain that they were included in the general term τὸν κόσμον τῆς μητρός, for Demosthenes states (46) that Aphobus took not only the cash in the house but τὰς θεραπαίνας as well. Wallon (op. cit., 240-43) has brought together evidence that slaves are frequently included in some general word meaning equipment, etc. Cf. also Thucyd., II, 14; VI, 91, 7, for slaves alluded to in connection with other possessions.

[53]XXVII, 13. Cf. supra, 51.

[54]Wallon (op. cit., 242) thinks that they were probably not more than eight or nine. Cf. infra, 97, 99, for the comparative wealth of this family.

[55]XXVII, 46: οὗτος τοίνυν καὶ αὐτὸς πρὸς τῇ προικὶ καὶ τὰς θεραπαίνας λαβών . . .

[56]VIII, 35; examples of Athenians mentioned with this same sort of an estate are found in Isaeus, VI, 34; XI, 44; Lysias, VII, 24, 31; XIX, 55, 57, 59; Demosth., XLVII, 53, 54; Diog. Laert., III, 1, 41-44; Aeschines, I, 97: "There was a house south of the Acropolis, a suburban estate at Sphettus, another piece of land at Alopeke, and besides there were nine or ten slaves who were skilled shoemakers" (Adams' transl.).

twenty minas, and the other, his private residence, valued at thirteen minas; besides this, slaves working for hire, and lastly, two θεράπαιναι and a παιδίσκη, with furniture suitable for such a house, these last three items being valued together at thirteen minas. His whole estate, valued at one and a half talents, not including considerable sums of money let out at interest, would place him in the class of Pentacosiomedimni. In this family then, and in others of a similar type, a menage of *three slaves* was considered sufficient to do the work.

Aristophanes affords several glimpses into the interior of Athenian households, perhaps less wealthy, but at least comfortably well-to-do.[57] In the *Acharnians* (about 425 B. C.), for example, Dicaeopolis (240 ff.) brings out his entire household in a procession to celebrate the Rural Dionysia. True, the celebration was theoretically being held in his native town, Cholleidia, but the exigencies of the theatre required that he merely turn around, enter his townhouse and come out with the household suitably arranged for the ceremony: wife, daughter, and *two slaves*. The internal evidence of the comedy would indicate that Dicaeopolis belonged to the Hippeis group.[58]

Fortunately Lysias gives a complete description of the simple home life of Euphiletus, who was brought to trial for the murder of Eratosthenes (about 403 B. C.). This gives a clear idea of how a certain type of Athenian family lived. In a naïve manner, the murderer relates, incident by incident, the events in his home leading up to the deed, how he had at first (I, 7) prided himself on having as a wife: πασῶν βελτίστη καὶ γὰρ οἰκονόμος δεινὴ καὶ φειδωλὸς ἀγαθὴ καὶ ἀκριβῶς πάντα διοικοῦσα. He gives the impression of having omitted no detail. He explains that he is temporarily occupying the upper apartment of his οἰκίδιον and allowing

---

[57]Other examples are Strepsiades in the *Nubes*; Trygaeus in the *Pax*; Philocleon in the *Vespae*.

[58]He was an important demesman of Cholleidia to be holding this celebration; he had eight drachmas in cash with him (130); his daughter was adorned with gold jewelry (258), and he describes himself as πολίτης χρηστὸς οὐ σπουδαρχίης. He does say (72) that he had lain on the ramparts in garrison duty, but hoplite service was not restricted to those of Zeugite census but to all of at least that rank. For Lysias (XXXII, 5) says that Diodotus went away as a hoplite under Thrasybulus, leaving more than seven talents of property behind him, which would clearly show that he was not one of the Zeugites.

his wife to use the ground floor to save her steps; he even mentions that he came in late from the country on the night in
question, inviting a friend, who had also stayed out there late, to
dine with him as he was likely to get nothing in his own home after
the usual dinner hour.[59] There figure in this story only *two
servants* (11, 12), the θεράπαινα who cared for the baby and ran
errands to the market, and the παιδίσκη who assisted in the general
housework. There seem to have been no men servants, for
Euphiletus, on discovering Eratosthenes in the house, had to run
to a tavern nearby for a torch and all around in the neighborhood
for assistance. Euphiletus may have belonged to the wealthiest
of the Zeugite[60] class but the fact that he lives in his own house
of two apartments, took frequent trips to the country, and mentions no trade, makes it seem much more likely that, like other
Athenians of the Hippeis group, he was living in town from the
income of a farm outside.

The wills of the philosophers,[61] transmitted to Diogenes Laertius
through some writer later than the fourth century, record quite
exactly the number of slaves in their estates. The slaves are
thanked in many instances for faithful services in the "Grove" so
that they could not all be grouped with slaves in domestic service
but represent the total number in the possession of wealthy men
in charge of a "school." Aristotle[62] refers to more than thirteen, of
whom he freed five, bequeathed eight, and there remained some
children whom he requested his heirs not to sell but to rear and
free as they deserved. To Herpyllis, the mother of his two
children, he left the choice of either of two houses completely
furnished (καλῶς καὶ ἱκανῶς) and three slaves, besides a maidserv-
ant and a boy.[63] Theophrastus, besides two estates, one at Stagira
and one at Chalcis, and the houses and the garden constituting the
"school," disposed by will of nine slaves, for he freed five, gave

---

[59]I, 8, 9, 16, 23, 42. One might infer from the latter detail that the friend had
no staff of servants in his house ready to serve him at anytime.

[60]*V. infra.*, 57.

[61]For a discussion of their authenticity and other problems connected with
them, see M. G. Bruns, "Die Testamente der Griechischen Philosophen," *Zeit-
schrift der Savigny Stiftung für Rechtsgeschichte Röm. Abt.* 1 (1880), 1-52.

[62]V, 1, 12-16.

[63]V, 1, 13.

away three, and had one sold.[64] Strato,[65] his successor, had six
and Lycon[66] had twelve. Plato,[67] in addition to two farms, six
minas of silver, jewelry, and furniture, mentioned five slaves in
his will. For men of so much property and engaged in directing
a "school," all the property of which was in their own name, this
average of nine or ten slaves apiece used for every purpose seems
significantly small.[68]

From the evidence of these families[69] and from the allusions to
the unpretentious style of living, I believe that I am justified in
concluding that a liberal estimate of the average number of slaves
in the families of the wealthiest Athenians during the fifth and
fourth centuries before Christ, those whose property amounted to
more than one talent and who thus were subject to service as
Trierarchs,[70] would be not more than eight or nine, and that a
large percentage of these were women. Also, that the average
number for those with less property, but yet enough to be included
with the Hippeis, might have been from two to five. Further, since
this second group was at all times larger than the first, I believe

[64]V, 2, 51-57.

[65]V, 3, 61-64.

[66]V, 4, 69-74.

[67]III, 1, 41-44.

[68]It is unfortunate that Xenophon (*Oec.*, VII, 3-6) does not give any numbers
for the slaves in the model household of the wealthy Ischomachus. There seem to
have been several, for a head-housekeeper is mentioned, and the duties to be required of the slaves by the young wife are listed. There is nothing, however, to
indicate that there were more slaves than were necessary in caring for such a
wealthy household. *V. infra*, 69 ff.

[69]There might well be included in this list of families that of the orator Aeschines
as described by a later writer in a letter purporting to have been written by the
orator from his place of exile, an estate near Rhodes (*Epist.*, XII, 11): "Here
I sit with seven slaves, two friends, my mother over seventy-three, my wife, and
three children." How much of his property he saved when he departed from
Athens is of course not known. The scholiast (Aeschines, I, 3) says that he owned
land in Macedonia, and Demosthenes (XVIII, 41, 312; XIX, 145) claims that
Aeschines inherited more than five talents from his wife's father, that he received
two talents for his work on the navy bill, and that his landholdings in Macedonia
and Bœotia brought him in annually thirty minas which imply an investment of
six to ten talents. (*Cf.* Isaeus, XI, 42 where a farm of 2½ talents brought in 12
minas a year.) At all events, seven servants for a household of eight free people
of whom one was aged and three were children seems a small number, when one
considers that this was one of the wealthiest families in the city.

[70]*V. infra*, 105.

that five could be reasonably considered as the highest possible average of the number of slaves employed as servants in the homes of Athenians considered rich by their contemporaries.

The other two classes of Athenians, the middle class and the poor,[71] may be discussed very briefly. According to the classification mentioned before (p. 48), the first consisted of those with a yearly income of at least 200 measures, or 200 drachmas in Solon's day, which later came to mean a capital of about 24 minas. This was a sum supposedly sufficient for owning a yoke of oxen, so that its members were termed Zeugites.[72] These were eligible to hold all offices except a certain few and to serve as hoplites in the army. The poor were all those of less property than the Zeugites; upon them fell no expense of services to the state, no opportunity to serve as magistrates, only the privilege of seats in the jury and the assembly. They were the dependent manual laborers called Thetes.[73]

We have little exact evidence about the home life of these two classes, but I believe there is enough general evidence from the two centuries to enable one to arrive at a rather definite conclusion about their slaves. First of all, Socrates is an example of a person who lived a self-supporting life on the scantiest means. All his property, according to his own statement, even if he could find a generous purchaser, would not bring more than five minas.[74] He had no slaves. Undoubtedly the overwhelming majority of those in the same financial condition had none either.[75] Some of the Zeugites, however, with as much as fifteen or twenty minas of property, probably, if they lived in the country, owned, besides a small farm, the span of oxen necessary for plowing and, in some cases, if fairly prosperous, a slave or two to assist about the

---

[71]Aristot., *Ath. Pol.*, 7; Plut., *Solon*, 18. *V. supra*, 48.

[72]For this view see Busolt (*op. cit.*, 191 ff.) and Gilbert (*op. cit.*, II, 145 f., 2nd ed.). Cichorius, however ("Zu den Namen der Attischen Steuerklassen," *Griech. Stud.*, Leipzig, 1894, pp. 135 ff.), argues that ζευγίτης used in reference to farming could signify only "yoked animals," not "an owner of a yoke of oxen." He regards the name applied to third property class, as related to ζυγόν, a rank in a phalanx, for all Zeugites served as hoplites. Pöhlmann (*Gr. Gesch.* (1914), 5th ed. 86 n.) agrees with Cichorius.

[73]Harpocration, *s. v.* θῆτες. Aristot., *Ath. Pol.*, 7.

[74]Xen., *Oec.*, II, 3; *Mem.*, I, 14: ᾔδεσαν δὲ Σωκράτην ἀπ' ἐλαχίστων μὲν χρημάτων αὐταρκέστατα ζῶντα, and VI, 1. *V. infra*, 95, note 5.

[75]Xen., *Mem.*, II, 3, 3; Aristot., *Polit.*, VI, 5, 11.

place.[76] Those who lived in the city, very likely owned, if they could afford it, a slave or two whom in addition to using in the house, they could let out for hire or employ in their own little shops, but it seems improbable that persons of this class would purchase and maintain many slaves exclusively to wait upon them at home, when possessed of no income upon which they themselves could live without work or remunerative investment of capital.

The "Cripple,"[77] with a property of less than three minas, applying for the state aid of one obol a day, claims that he has no one to assist him. It is unlikely, too, that families such as Demosthenes described in the oration against Androtion maintained any slaves to assist in the house. There the orator mentions law-abiding citizens who farmed, lived frugally, and were so short of funds at times that they had to suffer the deep humiliation of being seen by their wives scrambling over the roof to the neighbor's house, or hiding under the bed to escape the officious and odious tax-collector, Androtion, when he called to collect, insolently, the few drachmas they were in arrears to the state.[78] Euxitheus,[79] in the oration against Eubulides, very carefully describes his own mode of living to the jury voting on the question of his citizenship. On account of his poverty, his mother was then selling ribbons in the market, and directly after the Peloponnesian War had been reduced to taking a child to nurse. He adds, "And don't let it prejudice you against us, men of Athens, for you will find many women of civic origin taking children to nurse; I will mention them to you by name if you please. Of course, if we had been rich, we should neither have sold ribbons nor been at all in distress."[80]

---

[76]A poor farmer from Phyle (Aristoph., *Acharn.*, 1022 ff.) who comes upon the scene crushed with grief because of the loss of his two oxen (ἐπετρίβην ἀπολέσας τὼ βόε) is just such a person. He nowhere says that the Bœotians took a slave from him. The implication is certainly that he owned nothing which could be carried off but the two oxen.

[77]Blass, *Attische Beredsamkeit*, I, 633; F. H. G., I, 395; Philochor., 67, 68; Lys., XXIV, 6.

[78]XXII, 53.

[79]Demosth., LVII, 30.

[80]Other examples of poor hard-working families mentioned in literature and evidently without slaves in the house are: the public crier in Demosthenes' oration *c. Leochares* (XLIV, 4) who says "my father is a poor man and there are many like him;" and in Aristoph., *Thesmoph.*, 445-58, the poor widow with five children striving to earn a living by plaiting myrtle wreaths.

Poor families like these, of course, had no slave assistance at home. In families of less respectable reputation more servants were some-times found, it is true, than their income from invested property would warrant, but even in these, slaves are counted only by threes or fours. Demosthenes says disapprovingly of the notorious Neaera: "Neither Stephanus nor Neaera had any property to support their daily expenses; and the cost of their establishment was considerable, when they had to maintain their two selves, three children, two female servants, and one male attendant; and besides, Neaera had not been accustomed to live sparingly."[81]

Upon the basis of this evidence from the authors, I believe that the conclusion may be drawn that members of the middle class or Zeugites may have owned from one to three slaves employed, not exclusively in the home, but probably spending part of their time outside in gainful labor for their masters. In other words, families belonging to the class of Zeugites could hardly have owned, on the average, more than one slave used solely in household service. But the Thetes, who had no income sufficient to live without manual labor, must have relied wholly upon the free women in their families to do the work about the house.[82] They could not have had any slaves at all in household service.

In reckoning the total number of slaves used in this branch of work for all classes of citizens and for the metics (the foreign resident population), it will be necessary from this point on in the discussion to use the results of the investigations of others. There is considerable difference of opinion about the size of the free population of Athens and the relative number in each property class in the age of Pericles. But the figures of 21,000 citizens and 10,000 metics reported from the census authorized by Demetrius (317-307 B. C.)[83] have been quite generally accepted as indicating

----

[81]LIX, 42. *Cf.* the households of Theodote (*Mem.*, III, 11) and of Plangon (Demosth., XL, 51).

[82]There might also be included here as perhaps characteristic of country life in his own Attica the description given by Euripides of Electra (*Electra*, 70-76) performing unaided all the tasks of housekeeping in the tiny cottage of the peasant farmer to whom she is nominally wedded. Orestes (252) speaks of the house as though it were one typical of a working man: σκαφεύς τις ἢ βουφορβὸς ἄξιος δόμων and Electra replies (253) πένης ἀνὴρ γενναῖος.

[83]Athen., VI, 272 c. *V. infra*, 13.

a total free population of 90,000 to 100,000[84] for the last quarter of the fourth century. The other literary evidence strongly supports an estimate of about 20,000 citizens for that time.[85] To reconstruct the numbers for the last part of the fifth century and the early part of the fourth has been a more serious task and the estimates resulting from the newer researches vary from 40,000 to 55,500 for the adult male citizens and from 14,000 to 24,000 for adult metics.[86] Just as in reckoning the number of slaves in each type of family I have endeavored to give maximum estimates, so now I shall accept as a basis for further reckoning the totals for the free population given by Meyer[87] which are the largest given

[84]This is obtained by multiplying the number of adult males by three. Beloch (*Bevölkerung*, etc., 41-54) gives the most satisfactory discussion of anyone on the relative numbers in the separate age classes in antiquity. *V.* also *Griech. Geschich.*, III, 1 (1922), 270 f.

[85]In an oration probably delivered after 330 B. .c there is the casual remark (Demosth., XXV, 51) "there are altogether about twenty thousand Athenians (εἰσιν ὁμοῦ δισμύριοι πάντες 'Αθηναῖοι)." *Cf.* Plato, *Critias*, 112D. The story that the 160 talents confiscated from Diphilus (probably between 338-26) when divided among the citizens gave fifty drachmas to each citizen (Ps.-Plut., *Vitae X Oratorum* 843 D.) would show that the total number receiving the donation was 19,200. Furthermore, according to Diodorus (XVIII, 18), there were 12,000 persons disfranchised in 322 B. c. when Antipater limited citizenship to those possessing at least 2000 dr. and only 9,000 qualified. Plutarch (*Phoc.*, 28) corroborates these numbers. (According to Diodorus (XVIII, 74, 3) and Plutarch (*Phoc.*, 32) in 318 full rights were restored on the former basis, *i.e.* to all possessing 1000 dr.). Beloch (*Gr. Gesch.*, III, 1 (1922), 2nd ed., 273), I observe, in the matter of the Diodorus (XVIII, 18) evidence, now rejects the reading τῶν μυρίων καὶ δισχιλίων as emended from τῶν δισμυρίων καὶ δισχιλίων by Wesseling, defended by Grauert (*v.* Kallenberg, *Philol.*, XXXVI, 512) and confirmed by Plutarch (*Phoc.*, 28). Instead of 12,000 losing their rights as previously believed (*Bevölk.*, etc., 57), Beloch is now of the opinion that 22,000 fell below the standard of 2000 dr. But the second part to the third volume of his newly revised *Griechische Geschichte* wherein he has submitted the evidence for 31,000 citizens in 322 B. c., has reached me too late to include any extended discussion of that point in this study. At all events, should the proof offered be convincing enough to warrant the new interpretation as well as to increase the census figures of 309 B. c. from a total of 21,000 citizens to 25,000 as he proposes (*v. supra*, 31) there would be relatively only very slight changes to be made in the totals of the slaves as I am about to reckon them. The additional ten thousand citizens will have been added to the neediest group οἱ ἄποροι σφόδρα (Aristot.,*Polit.*, IV, 11) who evidently had an income of less than 240 dr. when 360 dr. were required to provide the necessities for a working man's family (Busolt, *op. cit.*, 203).

[86]Van Hook, *op. cit.* (1923), 80.

[87]*Forschungen zur Alten Geschichte* (1899), II, 148-96.

within the past fifty years.[88] In a detailed study, Meyer reaches
the conclusion that Thucydides' figures (II, 13, 6 f.), viewed in the
light of other substantial data,[89] warrant the conclusion that the

[88]Beloch (*Bevölk*, 73) estimates the population of Attica in 431 B. C. as from
40,000-47,000 free men over eighteen distributed as follows:

Three classes of Hoplite census	15,000-16,000
Metics of Hoplite census	4,000
Thetes and poor Metics	24,000
Total	44,000

Total free population 120,000-140,000. But *cf.* his remarks in *Gr. Geschich.*, III, 1
(1922), 273. His conclusions are accepted by Gilbert, (*op. cit.*, II, 202-3 (2nd ed.).
Francotte (*L'Industrie dans la Grèce Ancienne* (1900), 160 ff.) thinks that at the
beginning of the Peloponnesian War there were:

First three classes	20,600
Thetes	14,400
Metics	14,000
Total	49,000

Cavaignac (*Études sur l'Histoire Financière d'Athènes au Ve Siècle*, (1908), 174)
estimates the first three classes at this time as 25,000-30,000, the Thetes at 20,000.

[89]It might be well for convenience to list here briefly the few passages which
have furnished data for the many scholarly discussions and divergent views concerning Athens' free population in the fifth century. Herodotus (V, 97; VIII, 65)
gives 30,000 citizens as the estimate for his time; Aristophanes (*Ecclesiaz.*, 1133)
gives also this conventional number of "more than 30,000;" *Cf.* [Plato], *Axiochus*,
369A. Philochorus, Frg. 90, from Schol. Aristoph. *Vesp.*, 718 (Plut., *Per.*, 37) was
long the source of the belief that in 445 B. C. there were only 14,240 citizens, because
the statement is there made that 4,760 of the total 19,000 applying for a share of
the grain donated by Psammetichus were declared falsely registered and disfranchised
(*cf.* Beloch's remarks on this point, *Bevölk.*, etc., 78). But as Beloch (75 ff.) and
others have pointed out, this by no means proves anything relative to the total
population (*v.* also Meyer, *Forschung.*, etc., II, 178). Surely the wealthy citizens
did not stand in line for their bushel or two of meal, nor would the state normally be
providing food for those of Zeugite rating. It is clearly the number of the Thetes
at that time. Aristophanes (*Vesp.*, 709) also mentions 20,000 who would be
supported by the state on his plan. Further, a passage from Plautus (*Aulularia*,
107-10) it seems to me might perhaps confirm this view that only the needy took
part in any such distribution:

> discrucior animi quia ab domo abeundum est mihi.
> nimis hercle invitus abeo, sed quid agam scio.
> nam noster nostrae qui est magister curiae
> dividere argenti dixit nummos in viros;
> id si relinquo ac non peto, omnes ilico
> me suspicentur, credo, habere aurum domi.

As to the numbers in Athens during the Peloponnesian War, two groups of
statistics given by Thucydides (for his reliability, *v. infra*, 88, note 10) have been
the basis of searching inquiries, the details of which can not be given here. Im-

free male population over eighteen years of age in 431 B. C.
totalled, in maximum numbers, 69,500, distributed as follows:

Pentacosiomedimni and Hippeis	2,500
Zeugites	33,000
Thetes	20,000
Metics	14,000
	69,500

portant in summing up the conclusions of the newer researches are the essays by
Meyer and Beloch. The former (*Forschungen*, etc. (1899) II, 148-89) defends the
numbers in Thucydides, II, 13, 6 (corroborated by Diodor., XII, 40) as meaning
a total military strength among the three propertied classes in 431 B. C. (maximum
numbers) of 29,500 citizens, 3,000 metics (p. 162). This conclusion Beloch ("Griech.
Aufgebote," *Klio*, 5 (1905), 341-74) regards as entirely without foundation (see especially 359 ff. and 366) principally because of the statement in Thucydides, IV, 94,
that only 7,000 hoplites fought at Delium in 424 B. C. He would reduce Meyer's
numbers for 431 B. C. by at least 10,000. But if the context is more carefully considered, in my judgment, the facts given (IV, 93, 94) will not seem entirely out
of harmony with those of 431 B. C. (II, 13; 31). Thucydides relates that when the
city had been called out πανδημεί, metics, transients, and citizens (IV, 90) to
Delium, the Athenian army was face to face with 7,000 Bœotian hoplites, 1000
cavalry, 500 peltasts, and 10,000 light-armed troops (IV, 93); that the Athenians
had an equal number of hoplites and cavalry, but no regularly organized light-armed
troops. Thucydides further adds that *many times more* than the number of the
enemy had originally started from Athens, many without arms, but returning home-
ward left only the few to fight: (94) οἵπερ δὲ ξυνεσέβαλον ὄντες πολυπλάσιοι τῶν
ἐναντίων, ἄοπλοί τε πολλοὶ ἠκολούθησαν, ἄτε πανστρατιᾶς ξένων τῶν παρόντων καὶ ἀστῶν
γενομένης, καὶ ὡς τὸ πρῶτον ὥρμησαν ἐπ᾽ οἴκου, οὐ παρεγένοντο ὅτι μὴ ὀλίγοι.
Surely πολυπλάσιοι would imply that at least three times the enemy's 18,500
marched from Athens, or 50,000 to 60,000. Granting, even, that the πολυπλάσιοι refers
only to a comparison of the numbers in the light-armed forces (but Thucydides' words
do not indicate that) then it is safe to assume that from 30,000 to 40,000 of military age followed the 7,000 hoplites and 1,000 cavalry. Naturally, there must
have been some left to guard the city, perhaps some of the 18-20 and 50-60 year
old classes; other relatively small groups were then employed at other places in
the empire (v. Meyer, *op. cit.*, 158, note 2); the plague had reduced the numbers
by at least one-fourth (Thucyd., II, 58; III, 87) and three cleruchies had been
sent out: in 431 Aegina (Thucyd., II, 27); in 429 Potidaea with 1,000 colonists
(Diodorus XII, 46, 7); in 427 Lesbos (Thucyd., III, 50); 2700 according to
Thucydides (III, 50, 2). In 424, then, to judge from Thucydides, Athens may
well have had a total of 50,000 to 55,000 adult citizens and metics as opposed to
the 69,500 maximum estimated for 431. But the numbers of active hoplites
i. e., those still able to purchase their own equipment, had been greatly reduced.
Aside from those left on guard, or fighting elsewhere in the empire, there were
evidently only 7,000 (exclusive of cavalry) financially able to equip themselves,
and physically able to take part in a campaign, which is not surprising in view of
the events of the five preceding years. Several thousand, still nominally rated
as Zeugites, temporarily impoverished by being barred from agriculture, mining pro-

Multiplying by the usual coefficient of three to obtain the number of all ages and both sexes, Meyer then obtains approximately:

Pentacosiomedimni and Hippeis	7,500
Zeugites	99,000
Thetes	60,000
Metics	42,000
Total free population	208,500

As to criteria for dividing these into families, there is little or no positive information from the authors of the period. A friend of Socrates[90] complains of the hardships necessitated by post-war conditions of housing fourteen free people under one roof, but of course that gives little idea of the usual number. There seems to be no other way than to use modern statistics on this point. In the United States, according to the official census of 1920, there were on the average 4.3 persons to a family and 5.1 persons to a dwelling.[91]

Reckoning, therefore, approximately five for each family there will be obtained 1,500 families of the first two, that is, wealthy classes, and 20,000 families for the middle class.[92] From the

---

jects, etc., must have had to take their places among the ἄοπλοι referred to, unless friends could assist them. *Cf.* Lysias XVI, 14 for an example of such assistance.

After the terrible Decelean experience (Thucyd., VII, 27, *v. infra*, 83) and the losses in the Sicilian expedition (Thucyd., VI, 43, 94; VII, 20), it is not strange that in 411 (Thucyd., VIII, 65) there were only 5,000 with property enough to assist the state materially in war. Yet this did not represent the whole propertied class for in 407 Lysias (XX, 13) boasts that his client had surreptitiously enrolled 9,000 instead of the prescribed 5,000 as the active citizens fully qualified by property. These statements coupled with the fact that 5,000 were without land, hence almost any possessions, in 403 (Dionys. Hal. Lys. 32 = Argum. Lys., XXXIV), and that in the Corinthian War in 394 there were 6,000 hoplites, citizen and metic, and 300 cavalry (Xen., *Hellen.*, IV, 2), show how the numbers of possible slave owning families had decreased since 431. Throughout the following century they could scarcely have increased beyond 10,000 citizens, as the hoplites in the general levies would show (*v.* Beloch, *Gr. Aufgebote*, etc. besides the other more general evidence in note 85, *supra*).

[90]Xen., *Mem.*, II, 7, 2.

[91]*Statistical Abstract of United States* (1921), 61.

[92]A statement from Xenophon would show, in my opinion, that this method of dividing the total number of citizens by five to obtain the number of families gives a fairly accurate result.

Xenophon says (*Mem.*, III, 6, 14): ἐπεὶ ἡ μὲν πόλις ἐκ πλειόνων ἢ μυρίων οἰκιῶν συνέστηκε, χαλεπὸν δ' ἐστιν ἅμα τοσούτων οἴκων ἐπιμελεῖσθαι. In the context Soc-

approximate estimates given above of the number of household slaves belonging to each type of family as based on the testimony of literature, there might then have been employed in the families of citizens in 431 B. C.

$$1,500 \times 5 = 7,500$$
$$20,000 \times 1 = 20,000$$
$$\overline{ 27,500 \text{ slaves}}$$

But some of the 42,000 metics (a number regarded by Meyer, *op. cit.*, p. 179, as probably too high) must have had slave assistance in their homes. If we take into consideration that the metics

rates is giving advice to a conceited young man, Glaucon, who fancies himself at twenty qualified to govern the state (6, 1). By a series of questions he has shown the young man that the problem of governing a state is a complicated one, requiring much specific knowledge. No one can manage his own οἶκος, he tells him, unless he understands its needs and takes care to supply all that it needs. οἶκος is defined by Xenophon (*Oec.*, III, 4-10): οἶκος δ' ἡμῖν ἐφαίνετο ὅπερ κτῆσις ἢ σύμπασα, κτῆσιν δὲ τοῦτο ἔφαμεν εἶναι ὅ τι ἑκάστῳ εἴη ὠφέλιμον εἰς τὸν βίον. Now, he continues, as the state consists of more than 10,000 οἶκοι it will be difficult to provide for so many οἶκοι together, therefore, it would be a good idea to practice first on one, *e. g.*, the οἶκος belonging to Glaucon's uncle. The exact meaning of the word οἰκίαι has been a subject of much discussion. Wachsmut (*Stadt Athen*, I, 564, n. 2) and Beloch, (*op. cit.*, 100) have suggested, without entering into any discussion of it, that οἰκίαι probably here means households; but Wallon (*op. cit.*, I, 244) translates the word as though it meant houses and bases the estimate of the number of household slaves on this passage (*cf.* Hume's use of the passage, *supra*, 14). From this evidence he postulates 20,000 houses in Attica for citizens and metics and reckons two slaves for each house, concluding: "ce seraient déjà 40,000 esclaves employés au service interieur." Richter (*op. cit.*, 95) increases the number to 100,000, principally because there were many συνοικίαι where several families lived.

But οἰκίαι clearly does not mean the number of *houses* in the *city* of Athens but the *families* who comprised the *state*. This is a common use of the word in the sense of *familia*. *Cf.* Xenophon, *Mem.*, 2, 7, 6: ἀπὸ ἀρτοποιίας τὴν οἰκίαν πᾶσαν διατρέφει. Aristot., *Polit.*, I, 2, 1: οἰκία δὲ τέλειος ἐκ δούλων καὶ ἐλευθέρων συνέστηκεν. Also *Polit.*, IV, 3, 1 and *Ath. Pol.*, 20, 3: ὑπεξελθόντος δὲ τοῦ Κλεισθένους, μετ' ὀλίγων ἡγηλάτει τῶν Ἀθηναίων ἑπτακοσίας οἰκίας. So Xenophon represents Socrates as saying: this city-state is composed of more than 10,000 families (οἰκίαι); to manage the property (οἶκοι) of so many is a serious business.

The estimate of from 18,000 to 20,000 male citizens (Beloch, *op. cit.*, 74; Meyer, *Forschung*, II, 180) in Attica during the early part of the first quarter of the fourth century, when Xenophon probably wrote these words, would imply a total population of about 54,000 to 60,000. If divided by five there would then be 11,000 to 12,000 families, or expressed approximately, "over 10,000 families."

could not own land without a special ἔγκτησις γῆς καὶ οἰκίας it is not unlikely that the number of expensive establishments was smaller in proportion than in the case of the citizen population. Thucydides[93] mentioned 3,000 metic hoplites in 431 which Beloch thinks would imply at least a total of 4,000 adult males of hoplite rating.[94] Literary evidence shows that among these, as among the citizens, there were a few wealthy ones and many others in moderate circumstances.[95] There is nothing which leads one to think that the proportion of slaves used in the households of these 4,000 was any greater than that in the families of the citizens of corresponding wealth.[96] In the case of citizens, according to Meyer's estimate, the Zeugites outnumbered the very wealthy at the rate of almost fifteen to one.[97] This would give a total of 150 wealthy metic families and 2,250 families of the middle class, implied from the 4,000 metics of hoplite rating,[98] for which there would be reckoned: 150 × 5 =   750

$$2{,}250 \times 1 = \underline{2{,}250}$$

$$3{,}000 \text{ slaves in household service.}$$

This, then would give as a round number: 30,500 (27,500 owned by citizens and 3,000 owned by metics) for the number of slaves in household service when Athens had the largest population, just before the disasters contingent upon the Peloponnesian War.[99]

[93]Thucyd., II, 31.

[94]*Op. cit.*, 49, 71.

[95]Clerc, *Les Métèques Athéniens* (1893), 408 f.

[96]Lysias (XII, 6, 7, 8, 14, 19) gives data about the household of his father Cephalus. Several servants are mentioned in this. Callias, an aged metic, was indicted by his slaves (Lysias, V, 3). Poor metics are mentioned by Demosth., III, 56; Xen., *Vectigal.*, II, 3, 4.

[97]In the case of our own population the classification is sometimes made: Very wealthy 2%, lower and upper middle classes 33%, poorest 65% (W. I. King, *Wealth and Income of the People of the United States*, (New York, 1915), 78).

[98]4,000 × 3 = 12,000, the total number of metics of both sexes and all ages of hoplite rating. This would give in a proportion of 15 to 1: 750 wealthy, 11,250 middle class. The 750 divided by five as in the case of the citizens to obtain the families would give 150 wealthy metic families and 11,250 in the same way would give 2,250 families of the middle class.

[99]Beloch's (*op. cit.*, 73. *Cf.* also his statements in *Gr. Gesch.*, III, 2, (1923), 386 ff.) more conservative estimate of 15,000 to 16,000 citizens of Hoplite rating at this time and 4,000 metics would give a considerably smaller number of slaves. He does not state what proportion of these he thinks belonged to the Pentacosiomedimni and Hippeis groups. But Busolt (*op. cit.*, 188) thinks that out of about this

There remains the task of discussing briefly the possible varia-
tions from this number during the political and economic changes
of the next century. That there was a constant shifting from one
property class to another is to be expected.[100] As a result of the
losses of the Peloponnesian War, however, there were wholesale
changes in the personnel of the rich, the middle, and the poor
classes.[101] Over one-fourth of the population perished in the days
of the plague, the catastrophe in Sicily cost Athens thousands of
her population, the four successive Spartan raids had made many
of her wealthy land-owners destitute and had also made desertion
easy for the slaves. Numerous emancipations, it should be remembered, followed the battle of Arginusae. The Thirty are said to
have put to death more than 1,500 citizens, and their attacks
were directed especially against the wealthy members of the
democratic party.[102] In 403 b. c. there were 5,000 citizens who
owned no land at all, and therefore no houses.[103]

After the war, then, the number of citizens with income
enough to live comfortably probably never exceeded 9,000 to
10,000.[104] This is a decrease of more than two-thirds over the
estimates of Meyer for Athens in 431 b. c. As the total of slaves
owned, especially in the case of household service, varied directly
with the numbers and the wealth of the free, the maximum of 30,500
slaves arrived at for the period ending with 431 b. c. may well

number there were 1,500 in the wealthy classes. From these averages, i. e., 1,500
and 14,500, there would be, using the same method of reckoning, a little over
16,000 slaves.

1,500 × 3	4,500 total of all ages and sexes
14,500 × 3	43,500 total of all ages and sexes
4,500 ÷ 5	900 families
43,500 ÷ 5	8,700 families
900 × 5	4,500 slaves
8,700 × 1	8,700 slaves
	13,200 slaves
	3,000 slaves of metics
	16,200 slaves in household service

[100]Demosth., XLII, 4: "It is on this account that the laws every year allow
the tendering of exchange, because it is a rare thing for any of our citizens permanently to retain prosperity" (Kennedy's transl.).

[101]Xen., Mem., II, 7; Lysias, XVI, 14, XXV, 22; Thucydides (VII, 27) describes
the distressing conditions arising from the occupation of Decelea.

[102]Isocrat., VII, 67; Xen., Hellen., I, 6, 24; II, 3, 11 ff.

[103]Dionys. Hal. Lys. 32 (=Lysias, XXXIV, argumentum), cf. Thucyd., VIII,
65; Aristot., Pol. Ath., 29, 5.

[104]Beloch, Bevölk., 71 f. V. supra, 60, notes 85 and 87.

have decreased to 9,000 or 10,000. Towards the middle of the fourth century, as the city in general became more prosperous, so much so that men[105] like Isocrates and Demosthenes began to complain of the passing of the simple habits of men of the fifth century, the number of slaves in personal service doubtless increased from the lowest levels reached just before the Corinthian War.[106] However, the reforms of Antipater[107] in 322 B. C. revealed only 9,000 with property of more than 2,000 drachmas, that is, an income of 240 drachmas when 360 drachmas was considered necessary for a working man's family.[108] The census of Demetrius in 309 B. C. showed a total of 21,000 citizens and 10,000 metics.[109] At this time, when the number of those who were Zeugites or above was only one-fourth of that accepted for Athens in 431 B. C., even allowing for a growing tendency to a more luxurious mode of life that seems to have developed[110] at the end of the fourth century, but which, however, was never marked by much ostentation, I believe that for the families of the 9,000 to 10,000 citizens and the metics who had property enough to afford such a luxury, 12,000 to 14,000 is a generous estimate of the slaves in household service.[111]

[105]Isocrates, VII, 52 ff. Demosth., XXIII, 20 f.

[106]Beloch, *op. cit.*, 72.

[107]Diodorus, XVIII, 18, 5; Plut., *Phoc.*, 28. *V. supra*, note 85.

[108]Busolt, *op. cit.*, 189.

[109]Athen., VI, 272 b.

[110]Busolt, *op. cit.*, 199. *V. supra*, 48f.

[111]Of the 9,000 possessing at least 2,000 drachmas (*v. supra*, note 85) there were probably 1,200 listed as wealthy (*v. infra*, 105 and note 104). Reckoning as before (*supra*, 63-65), there would have been for the wealthy citizen and metic families (*v. infra*, 106 and note 106): 1,040 families × 5 = 5,200 slaves; and for the middle class, both citizen and metic: 6,759 families × 1 = 6,759 slaves. To this total of 12,000 there could possibly be added one or two thousand for those families who were not much below the property requirement of 2,000 drachmas.

[111a]This number may seem very small to one who recalls reading that a rich man sometimes had fifty slaves (Plato, *Resp.*, IX, 578), or that Nicias had 1,000 and Hipponicus 600 (Xen., *Vectigal.*, 4), both of course in the fifth century in Athens. But it must be kept in mind that Plato's remark included the whole number for every purpose in the possession of one of the small minority of citizens, and that Xenophon states that Nicias and Hipponicus invested in such numbers of slaves to rent them to mine workers at a fixed rate per day (*v. infra*, 89). They have no relation to the group of slaves discussed in this chapter. But *cf.* Moreau de Jonné's, *Statistique des Peuples de l'Antiquité* (Paris, 1851), 178 f. *V. infra*, 124 f. for an approximate reckoning of slave children, too young to be employed usefully, who have not been included in these estimates.

CHAPTER III

THE NUMBER OF SLAVES EMPLOYED IN
AGRICULTURE

No exact evidence exists upon the number of slaves employed in agriculture and there is, moreover, very little known about the methods of farming used by the ancient Greeks. Any number given, then, when so many of the essentials are still unknown, must be only an approximate estimate. But I believe that there is enough evidence of a general nature in literature to make possible a calculation that has at least some solid foundation.[1] Using the same method as in the preceding chapter, I intend to assemble some passages from literature about the rich, the middle, and the poor classes, as previously defined, this time the scanty evidence relative to the farms which they owned, and the probable amount of slave labor on them. Then, from the average number of slaves employed in these definitely known instances, I intend to estimate approximately how many slaves at various times during the fifth and fourth centuries might reasonably have been used with profit to till the farms of Attica. In all this reckoning

---

[1]Heretofore there has been more guessing about the numbers of slaves in this class than in any other. My two predecessors in this method of estimating the total by classes (Wallon, *op. cit.*, 246, and Richter, *op. cit.*, 96) have been content to dismiss this part of the subject in a single paragraph. They state, in brief, that most of the Athenians were interested in farming, that besides numerous small land-holdings, estates like those of Ischomachus presupposed many more extensive domains. Therefore, the 15,000 who owned land in 403 B. C. could well have employed 30,000 to 40,000 slaves on their farms, or 35,000 as an average. No mention is made for what period of Athenian history this number is to be accepted, but the inference is that it is to be considered an approximate estimate appropriate to any time in the fifth and fourth centuries. Glotz (*op. cit.*, 244) in three paragraphs gives a much more satisfactory discussion of the use of slaves in agriculture, but makes no attempt to estimate their total number. Heitland (*Agricola* (1921), 1-130) discusses the use of slave labor on Attic farms in a general way but ventures no estimate of the number employed. Orth (*Pauly-Wissowa, R. E.*, XII (1924) 624 ff., *s. v.* Landwirtschaft) gives no estimate of the number of persons required to till the farms of Attica, but expresses the opinion that (639) "die Bewirtschaftung der Bauernstelle war selbstverständlich Sache des Besitzers und seiner Familie, erforderlichenfalls wurden einige bezahlten Hilfskräfte hinzugezogen. Auf den grösseren Gütern musste sich die Tätigkeit des Herrn auf die Aufsicht der freien und unfreien Arbeiter. . . . beschränken."

the fact must be borne in mind that the Athenians were hampered by no conscientious scruples in employing slave labor, but were restricted only by the amount of their wealth[2] and the limited extent of the arable land.[3]

A great deal of what knowledge there is of the management of an estate among the Greeks is derived from the *Oeconomicus*, a treatise on household economy written by that enthusiastic gentleman-farmer, Xenophon, while living on the estate at Scillus presented to him by the Spartan authorities.[4] Whether Ischomachus, the central figure of the dialogue, is to be understood as a real person and his estate pictured therein as an actual reflection of conditions of land-owning among the wealthiest Athenians of the last part of the fifth century, or whether Xenophon is merely using this means of expressing his own views on what ideals a country gentleman like himself should aim at, is uncertain. There are traces of Spartan ideas[5] in the treatise, but making all due allowance for the part that theory plays in the account, I think that this dialogue is perhaps illustrative of the type of fine country estate just outside Athens alluded to by Thucydides[6] and Isocrates[7] as in the possession of the wealthiest citizens just before the Peloponnesian War, and re-established in part, no doubt, during the first decades of the fourth century. Ischomachus is represented as a very wealthy Athenian who at a short distance from the city owned an estate where he was in the habit of going in the early morning to superintend the work of his men engaged in farm labor.[8] The routine work is mentioned only in general terms and there is no indication of the exact size of the farm, whether additional helpers were needed during the busy seasons, or how

[2] The remark of Xenophon quoted in the preceding chapter is equally appropriate in this (*Mem.*, II, 3, 3): οἰκέτας οἱ δυνάμενοι ὠνοῦνται ἵνα συνεργοὺς ἔχωσι.

[3] See statement below, p. 82.

[4] *Anabasis*, V, 3, 7.

[5] X, 9, ff.

[6] II, 65, 2: "Yet in private they felt their sufferings keenly; the common people had been deprived even of the little which they possessed, while the upper class had lost fair estates in the country with all their houses and rich furniture" (Jowett's transl.).

[7] VII, 52: . . . "they passed their days in such complete security (*i.e.*, before 431 B. C.) that the dwellings and establishments in the country were finer and more magnificent than those within the city" . . . (Freese's transl.).

[8] VII, 3; XI, 12; 17.

many were regularly employed. But there is at least one slave overseer[9] and perhaps more, and the workers on the farm constitute a number of slaves for whom clothing, shoes, and maintenance in general must be provided.[10] Throughout the dialogue there is one fact emphasized, namely, that the successful farmer must have thrifty habits; he must attend to things in person and in time; he must train his overseer carefully to get the maximum effort from a minimum number of workers.[11] It should be noted that there is nowhere an indication of unnecessary laborers and that elsewhere Xenophon emphasizes this same point: "Every proprietor of a farm will be able to tell you exactly how many yoke of oxen are sufficient for the estate, and how many farm hands. To send into the field more than the exact number requisite every farmer would consider a dead loss."[12]

Farms of this type belonging to the wealthy families of the Athenians in the fifth and fourth centuries before Christ could not have been very numerous or very extensive in area. The comparatively small number of the wealthy, and the limited extent of arable land in Attica would preclude this possibility.[13] Alcibiades, described by Plato throughout the dialogue that bears his name, as a young man of extraordinary fortune, seems to have owned less than 300 plethra of land (about 65 acres).[14] Lysimachus, the son of Aristides, at a time when the city was "rich in land and in money" was presented with what was considered a very liberal gift: 200 plethra of land in Euboea (about 43 acres).[15] Granting that every bit of labor on these farms was performed by slaves in charge of a slave overseer, it is evident that no very large staff[16] would be needed.

[9]XII, 1-3.

[10]IX, 5; XIII, 10.

[11]XVI, 9; XX, 1-6; 15-21; especially (16): "Now it is of prime importance, in reference to the profitableness or unprofitableness of agriculture, even on a large estate where there are numerous workfolk, whether a man takes any pains at all to see that his laborers are devoted to the work on hand during the appointed time. Since one man will fairly out-distance ten simply by working at the time" (Dakyns' transl.).

[12]*Vectigal.*, IV, 5 (Dakyns' transl.).

[13]*V. infra*, 82.

[14]*Alcibiad.*, I, 123 D.

[15]Demosth., XX, 115; Plutarch, *Aristid.*, 27.

[16]*V. infra*, 84f.

From the last half of the fourth century there comes an account of another large farm, in fact, the largest of which there seems to be definite record in literature. A man who claims to have suffered ruinous losses in mining and other business ventures is bringing Phaenippus, owner of a border estate at Cytherus, to court on the proposal for an exchange of properties. The inventory, required according to Solon's law in a case of ἀντίδοσις, revealed,[17] so the plaintiff claimed, that Phaenippus lived on a farm more than five miles in circuit (probably not more than 600 acres in extent), yielding 1000 medimni of barley and 800 measures of wine yearly, and with timber enough so that six ass-drivers were kept busy, winter and summer, transporting wood at a net gain to Phaenippus of twelve drachmas a day. There were said to have been two barns on the place, each about one hundred feet in circumference. There is no statement, unfortunately, of how many slaves were owned to cultivate the farm, whatever its size. The six ass-drivers would imply six slaves, as theirs was regularly considered a servile occupation.[18] Slave-labor may be implied from the fact that the challenging speaker describes himself as a person toiling with his own hands for what he has, in contrast to Phaenippus,[19] but that may be only a rhetorical flourish. Clearly the plaintiff did not minimize the size of this farm or its yield, and it seems as though Phaenippus must recently have acquired this extensive property, or really have been greatly in debt as he claimed to be, or that the farm had no such yield, for otherwise with so much visible property he would not have been omitted from the list of the Three Hundred in the first place.[20]

[17]Demosth., XLII, 5, 6, 7, 20.

[18]Xen., Anab., V, 8, 5: ἀλλ' ἡμίονον ἐλαύνειν ταχθεὶς ὑπὸ τῶν συσκήνων ἐλεύθερος ὤν. Strabo, XIV, 2, 4.

[19]XLII, 20: πόλλ' ἐκ τῶν ἔργων τῶν ἀργυρείων ἐγώ, Φαίνιππε, πρότερον αὐτὸς τῷ ἐμαυτοῦ σώματι πονῶν καὶ ἐργαζόμενος συνελεξάμην· ὁμολογῶ. νυνὶ δὲ πλὴν ὀλίγων ἅπαντ' ἀπολώλεκα. σὺ δ'ἐκ τῆς ἐσχατιᾶς νῦν πωλῶν τὰς κριθὰς ὀκτωκαιδεκαδράχμους καὶ τὸν οἶνον δωδεκάδραχμον πλουτεῖς εἰκότως, ἐπειδὰν ποιῇς σίτου μὲν μεδίμνους πλέον ἢ χιλίους, οἴνου δὲ μετρήτας ὑπὲρ ὀκτακοσίους.

[20]The whole case of the plaintiff looks very suspicious; how could Phaenippus have concealed his property (a farm of 600 acres) from the officials who made up the list of the Three Hundred (v. infra, 105). How did it happen that the plaintiff had all his wealth tied up in mining property? It seems likely that he had invested in this expressly to avoid the duties of a trierarch, for the state disregarded mining property in averaging the amount of a man's estate for state duties. The area of the farm and its annual yield as stated by such a prejudiced authority should not,

Lysias, at the very beginning of the fourth century, gives an account of a smaller farm near Athens, on which, although the number of slaves employed is not definitely stated, any more than in the case of the two larger farms just cited, there is much information useful for forming a general picture of the agricultural conditions at that time. An unnamed Athenian, accused of having cut down a sacred olive tree, delivers the oration in his own defense. He describes himself as a wealthy man who had performed the services of trierarch, choregus, and so forth, more lavishly than anyone else[21] and, as Antiphon[22] remarked, that was a sufficient proof of a man's wealth. He claims that at this time he was residing on a small, treeless farm, the one in question, which was located on a main highway, unhedged from view, with neighboring farms on either side.[23] This farm, one of a number which he owned, he had bought directly after peace was declared (404 B. C.); he had rented it five days after purchase to Callistratus and after that to three others, before taking up his own residence there almost ten years later.[24] That he used slave labor on it is mentioned only incidentally.[25] He offers his slaves for torture and denies that his slaves cut down the tree or that the driver of the oxen placed the wood on the cart.[26] This would, perhaps, presuppose at least three slaves. Whether the persons[27] he rented his farm to used slave labor or not, is not stated, nor is it stated how

I suppose, be accepted as accurate or typical of many other farms at that time. But the amount of grain that it is alleged was raised there has been taken by several (v. supra, 23) as the principal basis for estimating a certain total grain crop and therefore, a certain population for Attica.

[21]VII, 31: ἐγὼ γὰρ τὰ ἐμοὶ προστεταγμένα ἅπαντα προθυμότερον πεποίηκα ὡς ὑπὸ τῆς πόλεως ἠναγκαζόμην καὶ τριηραρχῶν καὶ εἰσφορὰς εἰσφέρων καὶ χορηγῶν καὶ τἆλλα λειτουργῶν οὐδενὸς ἧττον πολυτελῶς τῶν πολιτῶν. VII, 21 : κατηγορεῖς ὡς ὑπὸ τῆς ἐμῆς δυνάμεως καὶ τῶν ἐμῶν χρημάτων οὐδεὶς ἐθέλει σοι μαρτυρεῖν.

[22]Tetralogia, I, 3, 8.

[23]VIII, 11, 24, 28.

[24]VII, 4, 6, 9, 24.

[25]VII, 16: πῶς δ' οὐκ ἂν ἦν ἀθλιώτατος ἀνθρώπων ἁπάντων, εἰ τοὺς ἐμαυτοῦ θεράποντας μηκέτι δούλους ἔμελλον ἕξειν, ἀλλὰ δεσπότας τὸν λοιπὸν βίον τοιοῦτον ἔργον συνειδότας.

[26]VII, 19: ὃς φησιν ὡς ἐγὼ μὲν παρειστήκειν, οἱ δ' οἰκέται ἐξέτεμνον τὰ πρέμνα, ἀναθέμενος δὲ ὁ βοηλάτης ᾤχετο ἀπάγων τὰ ξύλα.

[27]He says of them (11): ὑμῖν δὲ μεμαρτυρήκασιν οἱ πρότερον ἐργαζόμενοι.

his other farms are tilled. The inference is that he rented them
to independent farmers, as he had done with this one.

Like the father of Ischomachus, this man appears to have
invested considerable ready money advantageously in farms after
the Peloponnesian War, but unlike the former, who sold them as
soon as they were improved,[28] he rented his to free men who, because of financial reverses during the war, or for other reasons,
could not own their farms outright. I suppose that this man is
typical of many prosperous Athenians who were glad enough to get
back to little farms after the enforced stay in the city, and once
again to take active part[29] themselves in the farm work assisted by
a few slaves. From comedy one gains a more complete idea of
this group of citizens.

The farmers in Aristophanes' plays (beginning in 425 B. C.)
are not as wealthy as Ischomachus, or this farmer just described,
but they are comfortably well-to-do. Aristophanes represents them
as longing for peace and a return to their happy, active life,[30]
working out-doors with their slaves, ploughing the fields, pruning
the vines,[31] clad like the slaves in sheepskin coat and goatskin
cap,[32] punishing the slaves manfully for minor offences,[33] weighing
out their rations,[34] holding country festivals,[35] and making merry
indoors, slaves and all, during inclement weather.[36] There is no
definite statement of how many slaves each kept for his farm-
work. The household, inside and outside, is such a unit that it is
difficult to distinguish between those to be classed in household
service and those used exclusively on the farm, so that there is
danger of counting some twice. Dicaeopolis seems to have had two
slaves, one Xanthias and the other unnamed, perhaps a

---

[28]Xen., Oec., XX, 26: ἦν . . . φύσει φιλογεωργότατος Ἀθηναίων ὁ ἐμὸς πατήρ.
Πότερα δὲ ὦ Ἰσχόμαχε, ὁπόσους ἐξειργάσατο χώρους ὁ πατὴρ πάντας ἐκέκτητο ἢ
καὶ ἀπεδίδοτο, εἰ πολὺ ἀργύριον εὑρίσκοι; καὶ ἀπεδίδοτο νὴ Δί', ἔφη ὁ Ἰσχόμαχος.
ἀλλὰ ἄλλον τοι εὐθὺς ἀντεωνεῖτο ἀργὸν δὲ διὰ τὴν φιλεργίαν.

[29]VII, 11: Ἐπειδὴ τοίνυν ὁ χρόνος οὗτος ἐξῆκει, αὐτὸς γεωργῶ.

[30]Acharn., 32 f.; Nubes, 43 ff.

[31]Pax, 556, 566 ff.

[32]Nubes, 71 f.; 268; Vespae, 443 f.

[33]Vespae, 450.

[34]Pax, 1248.

[35]Acharn., 241 ff.

[36]Pax, 1146.

"Thratta."[37] Bdelycleon has Xanthias and Sosias on guard outside the house, but in an emergency summons Midas, Phryx, and Masyntias.[38] These last three were no doubt farm-hands, for in lines 443-47, Philocleon reminds them humorously of his kindness in furnishing them coats, shoes, and things appropriate for farm work and of flogging them carefully when they had been caught stealing grapes.

Farm owners similar to the one described by Lysias in the first part of the fourth century are found also in the last half of the same century. In the oration against Evergus and Mnesibulus, a rich man about to sail to perform the state duty of trierarch mentions his farm which was situated out near the race course, where he had lived from boyhood. The intruders, he claimed, had seized a slave boy in his employ and fifty sheep with their shepherd but the slaves working on the land had all escaped, some in one direction, some in another; there is no more precise statement than this of their number.[39]

Who attended to a farm when the owner was away on state or private business, together with other side lights on the owning of farms, is shown in the oration against Nicostratus.[40] In this, the farmer is none other than the wealthy son of Pasion, the banker, Apollodorus, lately honored with citizenship at Athens.[41] The

---

[37]*Acharn.*, 243: ὁ Ξανθίας τὸν φαλλὸν ὀρθὸν στησάτω. 259: ὦ Ξανθία, σφῷν δ' ἐστὶν ὀρθὸς ἐκτέος ὁ φαλλός. . . Θρᾷττα was a common name for a maid servant (see *Vespae*, 828 and Rogers' note) in the fifth century.

[38]*Vespae*, 433.

[39]Demosth., XLVII, 52, 53, 56. From the general description it would appear that the farm was not of any considerable size. The neighbors watch proceedings from their roofs (60) and Hagnophilus standing upon the land of Anthemion, a neighbor, watched the furniture being carried away and could see plainly enough to identify Evergus and Mnesibulus as the trespassers.

[40]Demosth., LIII, 4 and 5: "Nicostratus, whom you now see before you, men of the jury, was my country neighbor, and a person of the same age as myself. I had long been acquainted with him, but after my father's death when I went to reside in the country where I now reside, we were thrown still more together . . . he was of use to me in managing and attending to my affairs, and whenever I was abroad either in the public service as trierarch, or any private business of my own, I used to leave him in charge of everything on the farm" (Kennedy's transl.). In this case, then, not a trusted slave overseer, but a freeman, a neighbor, was left in charge and the orator mentions it casually as though it were no unusual thing to do.

[41]Demosth., LIII, 18.

action is taken against his neighbor Nicostratus in order to prove
that not the latter but his brother Arethusius owned two farm
slaves which should be seized to pay a debt to the state. They both
had some slave labor on their farms, for Apollodorus states (5):
"During my absence three slaves ran away from him [Nico-
stratus], from his own farm, two that I had given him, and one
that he had purchased."[42] But the part of the account most significant for this study is that the neighbor, Arethusius, evidently
a prosperous farmer (28), when fined a talent for his misde-
meanors, owned besides his other property but two farm-laborers,
valued together at two and a half minas (1) who could be sched-
uled for payment to the state. Cerdon he had reared from childhood
and Manes he had acquired in payment of a debt due him (19).
Furthermore, this staff of two slaves was let out for a fixed price
to assist his neighbors on their farms, for the orator says:[43] "I
will give you a further proof, men of the jury, that the slaves
belong to Arethusius. Whenever these men either bought the
year's fruits or engaged to reap a harvest for a certain sum, or
undertook any other farm service, Arethusius was the person who
made the purchase or engagement on their behalf. And this, too,
I will prove by calling the witnesses."[44] These witnesses, perhaps,
were the farmers living near by who, not wishing to maintain
slaves in idleness part of the year, found it more profitable to hire
additional ones at harvest time or other busy seasons; or possibly
that type of farmer is indirectly alluded to who tried to cultivate
his small farm himself, with only his family as helpers, and was
glad to sell his fruit crop or his grain *in situ* for a fixed sum.[45] At
all events the words imply that it was no unusual circumstance
for men under certain conditions to hire help from outside to assist
in farm work. Some farmers, then, did not keep slaves enough to
do all the work at all times during the year.

[42]The only clue as to the type of farm Apollodorus cultivated is in the charge
against Arethusius (15, 16): "He came at night into my farm, cut off all the
valuable fruit grafts that were there, and also the young trees in the shrubbery and
broke down the enclosed plantations of olives.. . . and he sent a young
boy . . . to pluck off the flowers of my rosary" (Kennedy's transl.).

[43]LIII, 21: ὁπότε γὰρ οἱ ἄνθρωποι οὗτοι ἢ ὀπώραν πρίαιντο ἢ θέρος μισθοῖντο
ἐκθερίσαι ἢ ἄλλο τι τῶν περὶ γεωργίαν ἔργων ἀναιροῖντο, Ἀρεθούσιος ἦν ὁ ὠνούμενος
καὶ μισθούμενος ὑπὲρ αὐτῶν.

[44]Kennedy's transl.

[45]Aristot., *Polit.*, VI, 13: τοῖς γὰρ ἀπόροις ἀνάγκη χρῆσθαι καὶ γυναιξὶ καὶ
παισὶν ὥσπερ ἀκολούθοις διὰ τὴν ἀδουλίαν.

There are few specific references at any time in the two centuries which I am considering to the farmers of the rating of Zeugites, that is, of the lower middle class, with an income from 200 to 300 medimni or a capital of 2,400 to 3,600 drachmas (24 to 36 minas).[46] But that does not mean that there was not a large number of such Athenian citizens living on their small farms which they owned outright, or had mortgaged, or had rented from the wealthier Athenians whose money had been invested in mixed estates. For throughout literature there appear in the background citizens of this type. Thucydides (II, 65, 2) for example, mentions them incidentally as having less to lose than their richer neighbors when moving into the city. The man accused of cutting down the sacred olive tree (Lysias, VII, 9 and 10) mentions Callistratus, Demetrius, Alcias, and Proteas to whom he rented his little farm before he took up his own residence there. Lysias (XX, 11 and 12) says that his client Polystratus, as a youth, lived in the country, without money, and tended his flocks himself; afterwards when grown to manhood he continued to work as a farmer.[47] In the *Acharnians* (1022) Aristophanes introduces a farmer of this class bewailing in pathetic fashion the loss of his two oxen. Whatever else he may have lost seems to have been nothing in value compared with these. The chorus of twenty-four sturdy farmers in the same play (208 ff.), principally charcoal-burners and vine-dressers, were probably not of higher rating than Zeugites. In the speech against the tax-collector, Androtion, they are described as "those who farm and live frugally, but through their having to maintain children, through domestic expenses, and other public burdens, are in arrears with the property-tax."[48] In the case against Eubulides,[49] some of them are present among the seventy-three citizens from the town of Halimus who have had to journey to the city to attend a meeting for the revision of the civic register, the majority of whom must hurry home before sunset.

Two farmers who claim to be men of small means[50] and should,

---

[46] *V. supra*, 57.

[47] ὃ μὲν γὰρ ἐν ἀγρῷ πένης ὢν ἐποίμαινεν . . . καὶ ἐπειδὴ ἀνὴρ ἐγένετο, ὃ μὲν ἐγεώργει.

[48] Demosth., XXII, 65 (Kennedy's transl.).

[49] Demosth., LVII, 9 and 10.

[50] Demosth., LV, 35: "I care not so much for the penalty (1000 dr.), hard as that is on a man of small fortune, but they are driving me out of the township by their calumny and persecution" (Kennedy's transl.).

perhaps, be classed with the Zeugites, are vividly described in the oration against Callicles. The petty quarrel over a water-course which Callicles alleged to have been wilfully diverted from its natural path to flood his land, is rather humorously set forth.[50a] The two, as their fathers before them, tilled their small upland farms, and seem to have had some slaves to assist them.[51] Figs, olives, grapes, and a few bushels of grain are mentioned as the year's crops[52] which might at any time be greatly damaged by sudden torrents from the mountains.[53] These men, as well as their neighbors frequently referred to in the oration, seem to have worked hard in the face of many difficulties to till their small farms and were willing to fight in court for every inch of ground.

There has been considerable discussion about the exact degree of poverty which Chremylus, the leading character in Aristophanes' *Plutus*, was experiencing.[54] The aged man (33) owns his farm (34), has one slave at least to assist him on it, and others in the house.[55] There is no doubt that he thinks himself very poor and unhappy at the present time, but the fact that he is so ill-

---

[50a]LV, 3, 4: "My father built the wall round this land, almost before I was born, in the lifetime of Callippides their father, and then his neighbor. . . . In all these years no one ever came to complain or object; though of course it rained then as often as it does now."

[51]LV, 31, 35: "And now he has himself obtained an award against me for non-appearance in another similar action, in which he made Callarus, one of my servants, defendant (Κάλλαρον ἐπιγραψάμενος τῶν ἐμῶν δούλων) . . . he has now himself procured an award in this other action against Callarus to spite me because I set a value upon the man."

[52]13: "There are trees planted on the ground, vines, and figs. . . . My mother having called upon theirs . . . told me what she saw and heard from their mother; that some barley got wet, about four bushels, which she saw being dried; and less than a bushel of barley meal; and a jar of oil, she said, had fallen down, but was not at all damaged" (Kennedy's transl.).

[53]10: "Between their land and mine is a road. A mountain surrounds both, from which streams of water run down partly into the road, partly on the lands;" 20: "Many persons ere now, I take it, have (for want of care) suffered by an inundation; and so has the plaintiff. But the worst of it is; he, when his land is overflowed, brings up huge stones and makes a dam; yet, because the same accident happened to my father's land and he inclosed it, it is a grievance, and Callicles brings an action against me. I can only say, if all persons who are injured by the flowing of water in that country are to sue me, I must have an immense increase of fortune to bear it" (Kennedy's transl.).

[54]*V. supra*, 18.

[55]26 f: τῶν ἐμῶν γὰρ οἰκετῶν πιστότατον ἡγοῦμαί σε καὶ κλεπτίστατον.

reconciled to this state and eager to do anything (but work) to improve it, might indicate that he is not entirely accustomed to it. And in fact, his own words seem to indicate that he is a farmer who has seen more prosperous days: (28 f.) Ἐγὼ θεοσεβὴς καὶ δίκαιος ὢν ἀνὴρ κακῶς ἔπραττον καὶ πένης ἦν. With his envy of those who are really wealthy (30, 31) and his pride in being thrifty, (245 ff.) and his love for riches which exceeded even his love for his son (250 f.) he is purposely represented by Aristophanes as proclaiming and bewailing his poverty. I think that he should be classed, even against his will, at least with the Zeugites. Some have affirmed,[56] using only Chremylus as proof, that even the poorest Athenian had one slave and perhaps more. They seem to forget that he is not an individual on the witness-stand, as in the orators, giving an account of his property to a jury composed of his neighbors, but a character in a play with traits purposely assigned him and emphasized by the playwright to achieve a certain effect. A trusted slave such as Cario, moreover, was an essential part of Aristophanic comedy. No slaves happen to be mentioned in connection with the very poor neighboring farmers whom he summons to his house.[57]

Whether all those of the rating of Zeugites used slave-labor on their farms or not, can not be answered authoritatively either way. The probability is, as the evidence seems to show, that after the two oxen, slaves were purchased to do the heavy work, if there was capital enough. For however small the owner's farm, slaves could be a source of income when rented out to his neighbors. Chremylus and his friends are not reduced to working for other people, as are the impoverished citizens mentioned by Euxitheus in the oration against Eubulides.[58] "Poverty compels freemen to do many mean and servile acts for which, men of Athens, they deserve rather to be pitied, than to be utterly ruined. I am told that many women of civic origin have become both nurses and wool-dressers and vintagers, owing to the misfortunes of the commonwealth at that period."[59] Euripides mentions three[60] poor

---

[56]V. supra, 18.

[57]223, 4: 255 ff.; 282 ff.

[58]Demosth., LVII, 45 (Kennedy's transl.).

[59]That is, after the Peloponnesian War at about the same time when the Plutus was given (388 B. C.).

[60]Electra, 78-81:   I at the dawn
Will drive my team afield and sow the glebe.

independent farmers (αὐτουργοί) at least one of whom, the honest peasant in *Electra*, tills his land unaided (71-76) by slaves. His reference to these as forming a distinct part of the citizen body may mean that there was some remnant at least, if not a considerable number, left in his day of that group of poor freemen trying by the hardest labor to eke out a living from the rocky fields, men whom Pisistratus strove to please in every way in the middle of the sixth century, and about whom there is definite evidence in the "Anecdote of the Tax-Free Farm" told by Aristotle.[61] There were some farm owners clearly too poor to own slaves.

With so few statistical data available, it would be useless to try to average separately how many slaves the wealthy, the middle, and the poor families employed in agriculture.[62] Small farms in the different villages of Attica seem to have been a popular investment[63] for the capital of the wealthy, but it cannot be assumed that these investors owned many slaves to till these farms. For it has been noted above that they might let these to free men who may or may not have used slave labor, according to their means.

> None idle—though his lips aye prate of Gods,—
> Can gather without toil a livelihood (Way's transl.).
> *Supplices*, 420 f.: "But yon poor delver of the ground
> How shrewd so e'er, by reason of his toil
> Can nowise oversee the general weal;" (Way's transl.).
> *Orestes*, 917-920: "To plead against him then another rose,
> No dainty presence, but a manful man
> In town and market-circle seldom found,
> A yeoman—such as are the lands' one stay—(Way's transl.)
> (αὐτουργός, οἵπερ καὶ μόνοι σῴζουσι γῆν)."

[61]*Ath. Pol.*, 16: "It was in one of these progresses that, as the story goes, Pisistratus had his adventure with the man of Hymettus, who was cultivating the spot afterwards known as 'Tax-Free Farm.' He saw a man digging and working at a very stony piece of ground, and being surprised he sent his attendant to ask what he got out of this plot of land. 'Aches and pains,' said the man, 'and that's what Pisistratus ought to have his tenth of.' The man spoke without knowing who his questioner was; but Pisistratus was so pleased with his frank speech and his industry that he granted him exemption from all taxes" (Forster's transl.).

[62]The metics are not discussed in this chapter because they could not own land without special permission. Xenophon advocated that they be allowed the privilege of owning one house and lot in the city, but there is no evidence that they were accorded even that right. (*Vectigal.*, II, 7).

[63]See Guiraud, *La Propriété Foncière*, 392 f; the landed property of Pasion amounted to twenty talents (Demosth., XXXVI, 5).

The evidence from the inventories of estates found in the orators would tend to show positively that these wealthy land owners invested in very few slaves for this purpose.[64] Moreover, a series of inscriptions[65] listing the goods sold at auction of eleven of the Hermocopids in 415/3 B. C. shows only one man, Cephisodorus, a metic in the Piraeus (who would normally be ineligible to own land) as the owner of as many as sixteen slaves. Of the others, though farms, oxen, crops, standing or gathered, and even one bee hive, are all listed as having been sold, only one slave belonging to Axiochus is mentioned. It might be, of course, that the state did not sell slaves as a rule but added them to its own body of public servants, but that is extremely doubtful. Yet, in another case of confiscation (Lysias XII, 19) slaves were turned over to the state. However, in the case of Pherecles, owner of several farms, the statement is made three times (100, vss. 22, 25, and 27) that the rent was paid ($\mu l\sigma\theta\omega\sigma\iota s \kappa\alpha\tau\epsilon\beta\lambda\eta\theta\eta$), so that these men whose goods were proscribed may have been in the habit of renting their farms

[64]There are many examples of this in the orators. The estate of the wealthy nonagenarian Euctemon (Isaeus, VI, 33) when converted into cash by the heirs brought a little over three talents, distributed as follows:

farm at Athmonon . . . . .75 minas
bath at Serangium . . . . .30 minas
house in the city . . . . .44 minas
herd of goats with goatherd . . . . .13 minas
one yoke of oxen . . . . 8 minas
one yoke of oxen . . . . .5½ minas
whatever $\delta\eta\mu\iota o\nu\rho\gamma o l$ (slaves for hire) he had . . . .————

The total is stated as: $\sigma\dot{\nu}\mu\pi\alpha\nu\tau\alpha$ $\delta\dot{\epsilon}$ $\pi\lambda\epsilon\acute{\iota}o\nu os$ $\mathring{\eta}$ $\tau\rho\iota\hat{\omega}\nu$ $\tau\alpha\lambda\dot{\alpha}\nu\tau\omega\nu$ $\mathring{\alpha}$ $\dot{\epsilon}\pi\rho\dot{\alpha}\theta\eta$. This would leave room for only four or five of the $\delta\eta\mu\iota o\nu\rho\gamma o l$ $\mathring{o}\sigma o\iota$ $\mathring{\eta}\sigma\alpha\nu$ $\alpha\dot{\nu}\tau\hat{\omega}$. Since $\delta\eta\mu\iota o\nu\rho\gamma o l$ is a word used of artisans (cf. Aeschin., I, 97) not farm hands, Euctemon, it is evident, had only one slave of this class, a goatherd. Similarly Ciron (Isaeus, VI, 35), with an estate valued at three and a half talents, owned three or four slaves for hire ($\dot{\alpha}\nu\delta\rho\dot{\alpha}\pi o\delta\alpha$ $\mu\iota\sigma\theta o\phi o\rho o\hat{\nu}\nu\tau\alpha$) but no slaves are mentioned in connection with the land he owned. The total assets of Stratocles enumerated by a certain Theopompus (Isaeus, XI, 42) to whose advantage it would be to give as large an estimate as possible, were five and a half talents. In the enumeration no mention is made of slaves on the farm which was valued at two and a half talents and rented for 12 minas a year. They might possibly be included in the statement (43): $\chi\omega\rho\grave{\iota}s$ $\delta\grave{\epsilon}$ $\tau o\acute{\nu}\tau\omega\nu$ $\kappa\alpha\tau\acute{\epsilon}\lambda\iota\pi\epsilon\nu$ $\acute{\epsilon}\pi\iota\pi\lambda\alpha$, $\pi\rho\acute{o}\beta\alpha\tau\alpha$, $\kappa\rho\iota\theta\acute{a}s$, $o\mathring{\iota}\nu o\nu$, $\acute{o}\pi\acute{\omega}\rho\alpha s$, $\acute{\epsilon}\xi$ $\mathring{\omega}\nu$ $\acute{\epsilon}\nu\epsilon\pi\acute{o}\lambda\eta\sigma\alpha\nu$ $\tau\epsilon\tau\rho\alpha\kappa\iota\sigma\chi\iota\lambda\acute{\iota}\alpha s$ $\acute{\epsilon}\nu\nu\alpha\kappa o\sigma\acute{\iota}\alpha s$, but forty-nine minas for $\acute{\epsilon}\pi\iota\pi\lambda\alpha$ (and it is doubtful if that word can be made to include slaves), together with cattle, barley, wine, and fruits, would leave only a small margin for farm-hands.

[65]Dittenberger, Sylloge, I³, 96-103.

to others who provided the labor to work them and that would account for no slaves being listed. These lessees then became liable to the state for the rent due the former owners.

In all the evidence that has been presented from literature, it has been observed that there is indication of some slave labor used whenever the financial status of the farmer permitted, but there has been no hint of any excess or wastefulness in its use, even in the case of the wealthy. Slaves on larger farms are probably so taken for granted that there is seldom anything but a casual mention of them. But many duties connected with farming were not considered "slavish;" as a whole, farm labor was considered healthful, dignified work suitable for free-born Athenians,[66] and there is ample evidence that the owner of a farm generally worked along with his slaves, or, in lieu of slaves, with his family. Moreover, from the nature of the crops raised, the work did not require any very great number of helpers all the time, but only at certain seasons.[67] At these times extra workers

---

[66]Xenophon (*Oec.*, VI, 4-10) concludes his eulogy of farming with: "Next we held it as proved that there was no better employment for a gentleman—we described him as a man beautiful and good—than this of husbandry by which human beings procure to themselves the necessaries of life" (Dakyns' transl.). Aristotle (*Pol.*, VI, 2, 1) discussing the best kind of democracy says: βέλτιστος γὰρ δῆμος ὁ γεωργικός ἐστιν, ὥστε καὶ ποιεῖν ἐνδέχεται δημοκρατίαν ὅπου ζῇ τὸ πλῆθος ἀπὸ γεωργίας καὶ νομῆς. *Cf.* Aristophanes, *Acharn.*, 32-36; *Pax*, 556 ff.

[67]Ciccotti, *Il Tramonto della Schiavitù*, 98: "In qualche regione del mezzogiorno d'Italia, dove la cultura de' cereali si fa senza sussidio di mezzi meccanici, e gli stessi animali sono adoperati soltanto per la trebbiatura, bastano da quaranta a quarantaquattro giornate di lavoro per eseguire tutto quanto occorre per un ettaro di terra, dalla preparazione alla raccolta. La contemporaneità poi de' labori nelle culture simili esclude l'impiego successivo dello stesso lavatore. La stessa coltura dell'olivo, piú persistente nell'Attica di quella della vite, a quanto possiamo dedurre dalla menzione ᴄhe si seguita a farne, non era tale de favorire l'impiego degli schiavi."

See also Cairnes', *The Slave Power*, (p. 51): "On the other hand, the cultivation of cereal crops, in which extensive combination of labor is important, and in which the operations of industry are widely diffused offers none of these advantages for the employment of slaves, while it is remarkably fitted to bring out in the highest degree the especial excellencies of the industry of free proprietors;" and (p. 62): "The successful maintenance of slavery, as a system of industry, requires the following conditions: 1. abundance of fertile soil; and 2. a crop the cultivation of which demands combination and organization of labor on an extensive scale, and admits of its concentration. It is owing to the presence of these conditions that slavery maintained itself in the Southern States of North America and to their absence that it disappeared from the Northern States."

were hired and the evidence reveals that both slaves and poor free men and women were hired for grape picking, olive gathering, vine dressing, and so forth.[68]

The evidence from literature also confirms the view that the land-holdings from our point of view were very small. Nine estates of wealthy men listed by the orators in the fourth century contain farms which sold for between twenty to one hundred and fifty minas (one-third to two and one-half talents).[69] Mortgage stones from twenty-one pieces of Attic property, some including a house, give an estimated average value of the mortgage as twenty-six minas. If the real value were twice that, the average would still be less than a talent.[70] The statement of a grammarian in the *Argumentum* to Lysias, XXXIV,[71] if accurate, gives the information that only 5,000 citizens (out of a probable 20,000) were without land in 403/2. Some of these, no doubt, owned merely a house lot in the city, but reckoning that 10,000 or 12,000 owned some sort of a farm, most of these must have owned only a very few acres, for the wealthy were but a small minority and the number of tillable acres was small. It has been estimated that not more than one-fourth of Attica's surface,[72] or in all about 150,000 acres, was tillable land. Now I believe that if for every fifteen acres besides the free labor employed there is allowed also one slave worker, or in other words, one slave to each possible farm owner, that the resulting total of 10,000-12,000 will represent in a fairly accurate way the maximum number of slaves who could have been devoted exclusively to agriculture during the fifth and fourth centuries.[73]

This number, of course, would have varied with the important political changes in Attica during the two centuries. In 431 B. C.

[68]Isocrates, VII, 44: Demosth., XVIII, 51; LIII, 20; LVII, 45; Aristoph., *Vesp.*, 711; Menander, *Agricola*, 45 ff.; Theophrast., *Charact.*, IV, 3.

[69]Collected by Guiraud, *op. cit.*, 393.

[70]See Busolt, *op. cit.*, 180, note 1; Dareste, *Inscript. juridiques*, I, 108 ff.

[71]Dionys. of Hal., *Lysias*, 32.

[72]Busolt, *op. cit.*, 180.

[73]This does not seem too small a number when one considers that part of these 150,000 acres had to lie fallow each year, since a regular rotation of crops seems not to have been widely practiced. Besides it should be remembered that not all the farms were cultivated intensively all the time. Xenophon writes that the father of Ischomachus made a business of buying run-down farms, improving them and then selling them for profit (*Oec.*, XX, 20-25). Aeschines (I, 98) refers to the farm which Timarchus owned and so shamefully neglected. *V. infra*, 99.

Thucydides described the Athenians as a country-loving people (II, 14): "The removal of the inhabitants was painful; for the Athenians had always been accustomed to reside in the country;" and in (16): "Thus for a long time the ancient Athenians enjoyed a country life in self-governing communities, and although they were now united in a single city, they and their descendants, down to the time of this war, from old habit generally resided with their households in the country where they had been born. For this reason, and also because they had recently restored their country-houses and estates after the Persian War, they had a disinclination to move."[74]

During most of the Peloponnesian War farming was somewhat irregular and in 413 was practically stopped. Thucydides says (VII, 27): "For during this summer Decelea had been fortified by the whole Peloponnesian army, and was henceforward regularly occupied for the annoyance of the country by a succession of garrisons sent from the allied cities, whose incursions did immense harm to the Athenians: the destruction of property and life which ensued was a chief cause of their fall. Hitherto the invasions had been brief and did not prevent them from gathering the produce of the soil in the interval; but now the Peloponnesians were always on the spot; and sometimes they were reinforced by additional troops, but always the regular garrison, who were compelled to find their own supplies, overran and despoiled the country. The Lacedemonian king, Agis, was present in person, and devoted his whole energies to the war. The sufferings of the Athenians were terrible. For they were dispossessed of their entire territory."[75]

The slaves of this class, then, must have been reduced to a negligible number during those days when successive raids made work futile and flight easy. One of the charges, too, brought against Megara, at the outbreak of the war, was that she harbored runaway slaves, presumably from the fertile farms of the adjacent Thriasian plain.[76] Thucydides estimates that, in all, 20,000 slaves

[74]Jowett's transl.
[75]*Ibid.*
[76]Thucyd., I, 139.

escaped in 413 B. C., most of them artisans.[77] If the number of those regularly employed in agriculture had been more than 10,000 to 15,000 in those days, it seems as though the total loss by flight from the mines, city, and fields would have been much greater, for many Athenians appear to have lost everything they owned outside the city.[78]

After the war it is doubtful if agriculture ever reached a stage of development equal to that of the prosperous days before 431 B. C. In the census of the land, houses, and all other property taken in 378 B. C. when the Athenians, in conjunction with the Thebans, were entering upon a war with the Lacedemonians, the value returned was but 5,750 talents.[79] From the census of 322 B. C., during the reforms of Antipater there were, as has been mentioned before, 12,000 citizens with less than 2,000 drachmas (one-third of a talent) of property.[80] Under economic conditions such as these which the statistics imply, and the literature of the period confirms, it is doubtful if the total of slaves on the farms was anywhere near 10,000, a number which would involve an initial expenditure of at least 200 talents. Furthermore, there is the indirect evidence from a Roman writer, two centuries later than the period under discussion, that this estimate of 10,000-12,000 as the maximum number of slaves ever employed in agriculture in Attica, is not out of the range of probability. Cato,[81] who sternly opposed the rise of the great landed estates of his day,[82] has left a classified list of workmen needed to operate two types of farms.[83]

---

[77]VII, 27, 5: . . . καὶ ἀνδραπόδων πλέον ἢ δύο μυριάδες ηὐτομολήκεσαν, καὶ τούτων τὸ πολὺ μέρος χειροτέχναι, πρόβατά τε πάντα ἀπωλώλει καὶ ὑποζύγια. For the reliability of Thucydides, v. infra, 88, note 10. Cf. Hellen. Oxyrnch. XII, 4 (Oxford).

[78]Xen., Mem., II, 7, 1 and 2; II, 8, 1-6.

[79]Polyb., II, 62; referred to by Demosth., XIV, 18. See Lypsius: "Die Attische Steuerverfassung und das Attische Volksvermögen," Rhein. Mus. für Philol., 71, (1916), 162 ff. V. supra, 21.

[80]Diodor., XVIII, 18, 5; Plut., Phoc., 28. V. supra, 60, note 85.

[81]De Agri Cultura, 10, 11.

[82]See Heitland (op. cit., 164-74) for an estimate of Cato as a valuable source of information about ancient agriculture.

[83]id., 10: Quo modo oletum agri iugera CCXL instruere oporteat, vilicum, vilicam, operarios quinque, bubulcos III, asinarium I, subulcum I, opilionem I, summa Homines XIII; 11: Quo modo vineae iugera C instruere oporteat, vilicum vilicam, operarios X, bubulcum I, asinarium I, salictarium I, subulcum I, summa

One hundred and fifty acres devoted principally to olives, he says, require thirteen people; sixty-two and a half acres, mostly in vineyard require sixteen workers; or a total average of one person to 7.3 acres. At this rate the approximately 150,000 acres of tillable land in Attica, if all cultivated to the same degree all the time and in units of 60 to 150 acres, would require only 20,548 workmen, free and slave. But considering the fact, that rotation of crops was practically unknown, that considerable free labor was used on the land at all periods, that there was a general practice of hiring extra workers from the outside during the busy seasons, that the unit of farming was distinctly smaller in Attica (where the average farm could hardly have been more than 15 or 20 acres if there were 12,000 farm owners), and that on the small farms little or no slave labor could ever have been employed, an estimate of 10,000 slaves as the maximum number would leave a wide margin both for any differences that there might have been because Cato was writing of a different country, a different time and perhaps slightly different methods,[84] and for the possibility that more of the surface of Attica than is commonly supposed was then farmed in one way or another.

homines XVI. In both instances Cato appends lists of animals and implements, etc. with which the farms are to be stocked. Varro quotes the passage and substantiates the numbers of slaves for farms of that size (*De Re Rustica*, I, 18).

[84]The Carthaginian system which Cato favored was one that distinctly required the employment of slaves, so that as between Italy and Greece the scheme of Cato would call for a far higher number of slaves than would ever have been used in Attica.

CHAPTER IV

SLAVES IN INDUSTRY

The slaves employed in industry may be divided into two general classes: first, those employed in the mines, and second, those engaged in any other gainful labor, with the exception of farming, which has been discussed in the preceding chapter.

The data regarding the mines which played such an important part in the economic life of Athens, especially during the fifth century, have been collected and ably discussed by Ardaillon, in a monograph containing the results of a first-hand study of the ancient mining district of Laurion, and an investigation into the methods employed.[1] Though his conclusions[2] may in general be accepted for the number of slaves employed there, it might be well for completeness to discuss the evidence again, for the tentative number which he suggests of 20,000 slaves during the fifth century and of fewer than 10,000 during most of the fourth century.[3]

The state[4] seems at all times to have retained the ownership of the lead and silver mines located in the southern part of Attica

---

[1] *Les Mines du Laurion dans l'Antiquité* (1897); see also his article "Metalla" in *Dictionnaire des Antiquités Grecques et Romaines (Daremberg-Saglio)*, III, 1840 ff.

[2] *Op. cit.*, 98-102, where he also analyzes critically the estimates of 60,000 by Boeckh, 10,000 to 12,000 by Letronne, 10,000 by Wallon and Beloch, and the reasons adduced by each.

[3] The chief sources of information from antiquity regarding the mines, aside from incidental references, are the oration against Pantaenetus (Demosth., XXXVII, about 347 B.C.)—a suit for damages from an alleged illegal seizure of mining property, and Xenophon's pamphlet on the revenues of Athens (*Vectigalia* or πόροι, written about 354 B.C.). Thiel's edition of this latter work (Vienna, 1922) with a commentary which contains many suggestions for the interpretation of puzzling passages, is the text from which I shall quote below, and the appearance of this very recent and thorough critique is my principal reason for weighing again the evidence upon this subject.

[4] It was not known even in Xenophon's day when the mines were first productively worked, for he says (*Vectigal.*, IV, 2): οὐκοῦν ὅτι μὲν πάνυ πάλαι[α] ἐνεργά ἐστι πᾶσι σαφές · οὐδεὶς γοῦν οὐδὲ πειρᾶται λέγειν ἀπὸ ποίου χρόνου ἐπεχειρήθη. From the early part of the fifth century, however, with the discovery of the rich new vein near Maroneia, there is evidence that they began to play an important part in the finances of the state. Aeschylus (*Pers.*, 238) says: ἀργύρου πηγή τις αὐτοῖς ἐστι, θησαυρὸς χθονός.

and to have leased large or small concessions in them, with boundaries carefully specified, to individuals, citizens, or metics,[5] on terms about which there is now no general agreement but which probably required as one condition that one twenty-fourth of the income be paid yearly to the state.[6] These lessees in some cases worked their concessions in person[7] with their own slaves,[8] or frequently with those hired from someone else, but in other cases they bought a slave overseer[9] to relieve them of any duties there. The important thing to notice is that practically all of the work was performed by slaves. No record has as yet been found of any free man being hired by another to work in the mines.

There is one rather definite clue to the numbers of slaves employed in the mines during the fifth century in a statement given by an historian who was on the whole most scrupulous in

And Aristotle says (*Ath. Pol.*, 22, 7): "Two years later, in the archonship of Nicodemus (483 B.C.) the mines of Maroneia were discovered, and the state made a profit of a hundred talents from the working of them" (Forster's transl.). *Cf.* Herodotus, VII, 144.

[5]Xen., *Vectigal.*, IV, 12: δοκεῖ δέ μοι καὶ ἡ πόλις προτέρα ἐμοῦ ταῦτ' ἐγνωκέναι. παρέχει γοῦν ἐπὶ ἰσοτελείᾳ καὶ τῶν ξένων τῷ βουλομένῳ ἐργάζεσθαι ἐν τοῖς μετάλλοις. It has been generally inferred from this passage that only a certain favored few of the metics could obtain mining concessions. (*Cf.* Glotz, *op. cit.*, 219: "Il n'y a qu'une industrie qui passe exception, celle des mines. Là il n'y a presque rien à faire pour les métèques: L'incapacité de posseder la terre entraîne celle de fouiller le sous-sol. Pour obtenir une concession, il faut que le métèque ait reçu l'isotelie, l'assimilation aux citoyens en matière fiscale.") But Thiel seems to have successfully established another interpretation of the words: "Ex hoc loco apparet peregrinos fodinas exercendas conducere potuisse ultroque iis isoteliam datam fuisse, *cf.* 4, 14 ad 22 et *I. G.*, II, 3, 3260 b (add.). Quod peregrini ἐγκτησιν non habebant, nihil ad rem: dominium metallorum respublica habebat. . . . ἐπὶ cum dativo pretium significat ut apud Plat. *apol.*, 41a; Thucyd., I, 143, 2, etc. Haudquaquam sub condicione isoteliae significat, quasi isotelibus tantum, ut metalla conducerent, res publica permisisset; metallorum opus enim sublevare, non impedire voluit; insuper, si hoc dicere voluisset noster, non ἐπὶ ἰσοτελείᾳ dixisset et τῶν ξένων τῷ βουλομένῳ, sed τῶν ξένων τοῖς ἰσοτελέσιν.

[6]Suidas, *s. v.*, ἀγράφου μετάλλου δίκη. Aristot., *Ath. Pol.*, 47; Ardaillon, *op. cit.*, 188-200.

[7]Demosth., XLII, 20; Xen., *Vectigal.*, IV, 22; Theophrast., *Lapid.*, 58; *I. G.*, II, 3, 3260 b (add.).

[8]Demosth., XXXVII, 4; 22; 26.

[9]Xen., *Mem.*, II, 5, 3.

the matter of statistics.[10] Thucydides[11] states that in 413 B.C., at the time of the occupation of Decelea, 20,000 slaves deserted, most of them artisans. The majority of those, it seems, were from the mines, for that is what Alcibiades (Thucyd., VI, 91, 7) had promised the Lacedemonians would be the result, if they should adopt his plan, and Xenophon (*Vectigal.*, IV, 25) dates the decrease in revenues from the mines from "what happened at Decelea." There is no way, however, of determining exactly how many of the 20,000 belonged to the mines, whether all who worked there then deserted at that time, how many had previously escaped when the Spartans in 430 ravaged the Laurion district,[12] nor how many had died from the plague. Xenophon, however, certainly implies that in those days there were more than 10,000, for to increase the present revenues he suggests[13] that the state, just as individual capitalists had been in the habit of doing, should buy slaves to rent to lessees of mines, at first to the number of 1,200, increasing that in five or six years to 6,000, and later to 10,000, when the income to the state would then amount to 100 talents a year. Even this, he adds, would mean operating the mines on a smaller scale than before the experience at Decelea.[14] Besides this

[10]Thucyd., I, 22: "Of the events of the war I have not ventured to speak from any chance information, nor according to any notion of my own. I have described nothing but what I either saw myself or learned from others of whom I made the most careful and particular inquiry" (Jowett's transl.); and III, 113: "I have not ventured to set down the number of those who fell, for the loss would appear incredible when compared with the size of the city" (Jowett's transl.). Also, V, 68.

[11]VII, 27, 5: τῆς τε γὰρ χώρας ἀπάσης ἐστέρηντο, καὶ ἀνδραπόδων πλέον ἢ δύο μυριάδες ηὐτομολήκεσαν καὶ τούτων τὸ πολὺ μέρος χειροτέχναι. These seem to have found refuge in Thebes (*Hellen. Oxyrhynchia*, XII, 4 (Oxford); see Zimmern, *The Greek Commonwealth* (3rd ed.), 402, note 1.

[12]Thucyd., II, 55: Οἱ δὲ Πελοποννήσιοι ἐπειδὴ ἔτεμον τὸ πεδίον, παρῆλθον ἐς τὴν Πάραλον γῆν καλουμένην μέχρι Λαυρείου, οὗ τὰ ἀργύρεια μέταλλά ἐστιν Ἀθηναίοις. *Cf.* Thucyd., III, 26, and Diodor., XII, 45.

[13]*Vectigal.*, IV, 23, 24.

[14]*Vectigal.*, IV, 25. If Thiel's emendation be correct, Xenophon is definitely stating here that the mines occupied many times more than 10,000 slaves in the fifth century. He reads: ὅτι δὲ δέξεται<τὰ ἀργύρεια>πολλαπλάσια τούτων μαρτυρήσαιεν ἄν μοι εἴ τινες εἰσὶ τῶν μεμνημένων ὅσον τὸ τέλος εὕρισκε τῶν ἀνδραπόδων πρὸ τῶν ἐν Δεκελείᾳ with the comment, "Haec non significant: aerarium multo plus centum talentis accipiet, sed: metalla multo maiorem numerum servorum quam decem milia capient . . verba τὰ ἀργύρεια igitur (25 v. 2) prorsus supervacanea huc transposui ne verbum δέξεται subiecto careret; suspicor τὰ ἀργύρεια forte omissum in margine postea additum fuisse et deinde alieno loco insertum."

it should be noted that Xenophon nowhere advocates that the state
with this number of 10,000 should entirely supplant private ownership of slaves for this purpose, so that there would be others employed there besides these. Yet, taken as a whole, there is nothing
about his scheme which would indicate that there had been in the
fifth century, or at any time, as many as 50,000 or 60,000 slaves in
the mines,[15] as has been conjectured from his chance remark at
the outset that Athens should aim to develop its mines to their
utmost capacity, and should ultimately strive to reach the goal of
owning three such slaves for every citizen.[16] It is significant that
he does not take time to estimate a future income from more than
10,000, which would hardly have been the case if five or six times
that number had been employed there less than a century before.
That he cites in support of the feasibility of his plan the fact that
in the fifth century Nicias[17] owned 1,000 slaves whom he rented
to Sosias, the Thracian, for an obol a day net, that Hipponicus for
similar terms rented 600 and Philemonides 300 (numbers which
have been often quoted to show that the Athenians owned myriads
of slaves), is not evidence that many others at the same time
owned anything approximating that number. These he mentions
as extraordinary cases, the fame of which had lasted nearly a

---

[15]Boeckh, *op. cit.* (3rd ed.), I, 52.

[16]IV, 18; Richter, *op. cit.*, 97; *v. supra*, 25. The optimistic Xenophon also
dreams that in the days to come when there are possibly three slaves per citizen
owned by the state and employed at Laurion, then house lots near the mines will
sell for as much as those in the suburbs of Athens (IV, 50): ἰσχυρῶς γὰρ <ἂν> καὶ
αὕτη πολυάνθρωπος γένοιτο πόλις εἰ οὕτω κατασκευασθείη. καὶ οἱ γε χῶροι οὐδὲν
ἂν εἶεν μείονος ἄξιοι τοῖς κεκτημένοις ἐνταῦθα ἢ τοῖς περὶ τὸ ἄστυ. But no one, as
yet, has used this remark as proof that such actually was the value of the barren
land about Laurion in the fifth century!

[17]IV, 14: There has been some question as to whether Nicias owned these
1,000 slaves in addition to those which he was known to have employed himself in
his own mines (Plut., *Nic. et Crassus*, 4, 2) and for whom he bought an overseer
(ἐπιστάτης) for a talent (Xen., *Mem.*, II, 5, 2). Thiel, in a note to the passage,
reconciles the three pieces of evidence in a manner which is probably correct:
"Σωσίας noster idem homo est atque ἐπιστάτης ille. Quem operis metallici per-
itum emit Nicias, ut servum operibus suis quae suo periculo etiam tum exerceret,
praeficeret. Postea, cum opus magnum suo periculo exercere Niciam taederet
neque iam per rem publicam ipsum regere vacaret, Sosiae manumisso fodinas suas
ipsius periculo exercendas tradidit . . . Inde ab eo tempore igitur Sosias
libertus et inquilinus suo sumptu et sui iuris opus exercuit."

hundred years.[18] The last part of his statement in this connection is more important (though seldom quoted) in giving an idea of the actual status of the matter, "and the others, I suppose, owned such slaves, each according to his means."[19] That it was usual for many of the others to have owned just one slave working in the mines, is to be inferred from the incidental, and therefore valuable, allusion to the subject found in Andocides, I, 38. Dioclides, with the help of Alcibiades, had devised a plausible story to tell the council investigating the Hermes' scandal (414 B. C.) to account for his having seen in the moonlight 300 citizens and metics plotting mischief to the images. Andocides reports: "He said that he had a *slave* at Laurion so he had to go down to collect the rent for him, that by mistake he arose earlier than he had planned and started out; it was bright moonlight."[20]

In view of the evidence then, it is certain that in the hey-day of the mining industry, before 430 B. C., more than 10,000 slaves were employed by citizens and metics in the work above and below the ground, and that very likely the total for a short time was not far from 20,000.[21]

Throughout the literature of the first half of the fourth century there are echoes of the continued decrease in the output of the

[18]IV, 14: πάλαι μὲν γὰρ δήπου οἷς μεμέληκεν ἀκηκόαμεν ὅτι Νικίας . . . κτλ. Besides, 1000, 600, 300 are probably mere round numbers as the Greeks and Romans so frequently used them. See Pease on Cic., *De Divinatione* (1923), II, 34.

[19](15): ἄλλοις δέ γε ὡς, οἴομαι, δύναμις ἑκάστοις ὑπῆρχεν.

[20]ἔφη γὰρ εἶναι μὲν ἀνδράποδόν οἱ ἐπὶ Λαυρίῳ, δεῖν δὲ κομίσασθαι ἀποφοράν. ἀναστὰς δὲ πρῲ ψευσθεὶς τῆς ὥρας βαδίζειν· εἶναι δὲ πανσέληνον.

[21]With Ardaillon's conclusion (p. 100) I can agree: "Ce que nous pouvons affirmer, c'est qu'avant cet événement, les esclaves étaient beaucoup plus nombreux au Laurion qu'ils ne l'étaient au moment où Xénophon écrivait, et que leur total dépassait alors 10,000. . . . D'autre part, si l'on considère la population qui habite de nos jours le Laurion et l'importance des travaux en cours, on arrivera à une conclusion analogue à celle qui se dégage du texte de Xénophon. . . . A supposer que les travaux n'aient pas eu plus d'extension et d'importance qu'ils n'en ont aujourd'hui, ce qui est peu probable, nous sommes, je crois, en droit d'affirmer qu'à l'époque de Périclès, la population du Laurion dépassait le chiffre de 20,000 âmes; car ce n'est pas tomber dans l'exagération que de doubler les chiffres actuels, si l'on songe que le travail, accompli de nos jours par de nombreuses machines à vapeur, était alors exécuté par des hommes."

The *Handbook of Greece* (1920), Vol. I, p. 216 states (*s. r.* Laurion): "Lead mines and smelting works (French and Greek companies). Population 11,600."

mines first occasioned by the Peloponnesian War.[22] In 405 Aristophanes[23] scoffs at the new bronze coinage, issued no doubt because of the lack of silver; in 387 there is the same complaint of the scarcity of silver.[24] A little later Isocrates[25] mourns the fact that wealthy citizens, harassed by continuous wars and heavy state burdens, have had no chance to replenish their exhausted resources; Socrates is represented by Xenophon[26] as inquiring of Glaucon, the youthful aspirant to a political career, whether he could explain why the mines were less productive than formerly. Xenophon (about 354) answers the question himself:[27] "To open cuttings in new directions today is just as possible as it was in former times. . . . Well then, it may be asked why it is that there is not the same rush to make new cuttings now as in former times? The answer is, because the people concerned with the mines are poorer nowadays. The attempt to restart operations, renew plants, etc., is of recent date, and any one who ventures to open up a new area runs a considerable risk. Supposing he hits upon a productive field, he becomes a rich man, but supposing he draws a blank, he loses the whole of his outlay; and that is a danger which people of the present time are shy of facing."[28]

A revival of interest in mining investments was beginning about the time that Xenophon wrote this treatise (he explicitly remarks, νεωστὶ γὰρ πάλιν κατασκευάζονται),[29] and seems to have reached some degree of success when the state was under the management of Eubulus and Lycurgus. Xenophon's plan had involved cooperation on the part of the tribes (IV, 30) in bearing the expenses of

---

[22]See references cited above, p. 88.

[23]*Ran.*, 720 ff. with *schol.* to passage; see Rogers' note to the lines. Thiel (*op. cit.*, Excursus, XI) calls attention to the fact that the price of lead more than doubled at that time. Aristot., *Oec.*, II, 2, 36; *I. G.*, II, 834b, 40; I, 324c, 38-41.

[24]Lysias, XIX, 11.

[25]VIII, 128, 131.

[26]*Mem.*, III, 6, 12: εἰς γε μὴν, ἔφη, τ'ἀργύρεια οἶδ' ὅτι οὐκ ἀφῖξαι, ὥστ' ἔχειν εἰπεῖν δι' ὅτι νῦν ἐλάττω ἢ πρόσθεν προσέρχεται αὐτόθεν.

[27]*Vectigal.*, IV, 28: τί δῆτα, φαίη ἂν τις, οὐ καὶ νῦν, ὥσπερ ἔμπροσθεν, πολλοὶ καινοτομοῦσιν; ὅτι πενέστεροι μὲν νῦν εἰσιν οἱ περὶ τὰ μέταλλα· (νεωστὶ γὰρ πάλιν κατασκευάζονται). κίνδυνος δὲ μέγας τῷ καινοτομοῦντι· ὁ μὲν γὰρ εὑρὼν ἀγαθὴν ἐργασίην πλούσιος γίγνεται, ὁ δὲ μὴ εὑρὼν πάντα ἀπόλλυσιν ὅσα ἂν δαπανήσῃ. εἰς τοῦτον οὖν τὸν κίνδυνον οὐ μάλα πως ἐθέλουσιν οἱ νῦν ἰέναι. See also Thiel's note to this passage.

[28]Dakyns' transl.

[29]See passage just cited.

making new cuttings. A modified form of the plan seems to have been adopted, for the successful investors in mining stock, of whom there is mention in this period, appear to have pooled their interests in some sort of organized companies.[30]

There is a complete lack of statistical evidence for the total number of slaves employed in the mines during this period.[31] Xenophon[32] could say in 354 B. C.: "and now there are many men in the silver mines hired under the same conditions" [i.e., as those belonging to Nicias]. But how many are πολλοί? No exact answer can be given as yet. His whole account would indicate that the number was far less than in the fifth century and the necessity which he feels himself under to encourage his readers in every possible way to believe that 1,200 slaves could be bought and put to work in the mines and very gradually the number increased to as many as 10,000, would show that there were less than 10,000 there in his day. Beloch[33] is of the opinion that there

---

[30]Demosth., XXXVII, 38; XLII, 3; Hyperid., frg. *pro Lycophr.*, Col. 2 (Oxford); Hyperid. frg. *pro Euxenippo*, Col. 26-30 (Oxford), especially (col. 27: φήναντος γὰρ Λυσάνδρου τὸ Ἐπικράτους μέταλλον τοῦ Παλληνέως <ὡς> ἐντὸς τῶν μέτρων τετμημένον, ὃ ἠργάζετο μὲν ἤδη τρία ἔτη, μετεῖχον δ' αὐτοῦ οἱ πλουσιώτατοι σχεδόν τι τῶν ἐν τῇ πόλει, ὁ δὲ Λύσανδρος ὑπισχνεῖτο τριακόσια τάλαντα εἰσ[πράξει]ν τῇ πόλει τ[οσαῦτα] γὰρ εἰληφέναι α[ὐτοὺς] ἐκ τοῦ μετάλλου). And I suspect that in the case of Diphilus, condemned to death in the time of Lycurgus for having encroached upon the pillars in his mining, his fortune of 160 talents, reputed to have been confiscated and distributed among the citizens (*v. supra*, 60, note 85), really represented the total assets of Diphilus & Co. The silent partners in the firm would not have cared to make themselves known under the circumstances. Such a private fortune is unparalleled for those times in Attica though often quoted (Boeckh, *op. cit.*, 3rd ed., 570) as an example of the fortunes of that age, and to whomever it belonged it was amassed and dissipated over night, so to speak. (*Cf.* Aristot., *Pol.*, I, 4, 7 for the summary punishment of another speculator, this time in iron.) The story is found in (Plut.) *Vitae X, Oratorum, Lycurg.*, 843 D: ἔκρινε (*sc.* Lycurgus) δὲ καὶ Δίφιλον ἐκ τῶν ἀργυρείων μετάλλων τοὺς μεσοκρινεῖς, οἳ ἐβάσταζον τὰ ὑπερκείμενα βάρη, ὑφελόντα καὶ ἐξ αὐτῶν πεπλουτηκότα παρὰ τοὺς νόμους· καὶ θανάτου ὄντος ἐπιτιμίου ἀλῶναι ἐποίησε καὶ πεντήκοντα δραχμὰς ἐκ τῆς οὐσίας αὐτοῦ ἑκάστῳ τῶν πολιτῶν διένειμε, τῶν πάντων συναχθέντων ταλάντων ἑκατὸν ἑξήκοντα· ἤ, ὥς τινες, μνᾶν.

[31]With thirty slaves Pantaenetus works a concession valued at a talent (Demosth., XXXVII, 4, 5) but there is no knowing whether he is a typical lessee, and if so, how many others like him there were. Timarchus, we also know (Aeschin., I, 101) inherited two concessions in the mines (ἐργαστήρια δύο ἐν τοῖς ἀργυρείοις).

[32]*Vectigal.*, IV, 17: καὶ γὰρ νῦν πολλοὶ εἰσιν ἐν τοῖς ἀργυρείοις ἄνθρωποι οὕτως ἐκδεδομένοι.

[33]*Op. cit.*, 94.

were about 5,000 employed at Laurion during the first half of the fourth century, a number which, in my opinion, the general evidence would tend to support.

The boom beginning with the middle of the fourth century seems to have been but a temporary one, and for various reasons, not to have reached the heights of the one a hundred years earlier, chiefly, I suppose, from lack of capital and changed political conditions. The opponent of Phaenippus (Demosth., XLII, 3) says (about 330 B.C.): "*I have shared the general misfortunes of all those engaged in the works,* and have also incurred special losses of a ruinous nature in my own business, and now on this last occasion I have to pay the state three talents, a talent for every share . . . for I was a partner, I am sorry to say, in the confiscated mine."[34] The history of the bronze coinage in Athens, too, throws some light on conditions in the silver mines. Attic silver coins were plentiful and in wide circulation during most of the fifth century. Makeshift bronze coins had to be issued in 405 B.C. (see above, p. 91 and note) when Athens found herself in such desperate financial straits, but were in circulation only until Conon's victory in 394 B.C. Then the Town Crier was sent around to proclaim the joyful news that silver was once more to be the only legal tender. Yet silver coins seem to have been far from plentiful because about 339 B.C. the state had to resort to another bronze coinage.[35] In view of these considerations, I believe that the slaves employed in the mines during the latter half of the fourth century were considerably fewer than in the fifth century and can be safely estimated as numbering somewhere between 5,000 and 10,000.

The silver mines, it might be added, seem to have suffered a steady decline from this time on for Diodorus[36] reports that two centuries later the slaves who revolted at Laurion, in the great uprising of 104 B.C. when the events in Sicily were arousing the servile population everywhere, numbered only 1,000;[37] while

---

[34]Kennedy's transl.

[35]See Head, *Historia Numorum* (1911), 373-77.

[36]XXXIV, 2, 19.

[37]*Cf.* Oros., V, 9; Athen., VI, 272 e; this seems to be the only real revolt of slaves recorded for Attica. The desertion of 20,000 in 413 B.C. was deliberately instigated by the enemy. This in itself is no slight indication that probably there were never many myriads of slaves at any one time working in the mines, or

Strabo in the first century of the Christian era, went so far as to say: "the silver mines in Attica at first were of some consequence but now they are exhausted."[38]

There remains to be discussed the number of slaves employed in all the rest of industry as defined at the beginning of this chapter. It would be useless to attempt to count all the different gainful occupations in which slaves took part. Literature shows them as assistants to bakers, tailors, grocers, tanners, druggists, bankers, physicians, manufacturers of armor, of ready made clothing and of furniture, and to a host of other business people.[39] At times slaves are found occupying very responsible positions such as the proprietor of a shop,[40] the foreign agent of an importing firm,[41] or the director of a bank;[42] at other times they are merely waiting around in the Piraeus on the chance of earning an obol or two by running on errands for a newly arrived foreigner.[43] In short, the occupation of the slave depended largely on that of his master.[44] But often citizens with capital to invest, even though they themselves were not actively interested in business, bought workmen who could be hired out to other persons at a fixed

their discontent would have manifested itself at some time, for the working conditions were recognized as distinctly bad even by the ancients themselves. Theophrast., *Lapid.*, 63; Plut., *Nic. et Crass.*, I, 1; Diodor., V, 28; Xen., *Mem.*, III, 6, 12. The galleries in which the slaves worked were not more than three to five feet wide and high so that they had to lie on their backs or crouch on their knees all the time. The system of ventilation was inadequate and oil lamps vitiated the air. For these reasons, only the lowest class of slaves was used for this work. See Ardaillon, *op. cit.*, 21 ff., 94 ff.

[38]IX, 23: τὰ δ' ἀργύρεια τὰ ἐν τῇ Ἀττικῇ κατ' ἀρχὰς μὲν ἦν ἀξιόλογα, νυνὶ δ' ἐκλείπει.

[39]Xen., *Mem.*, II, 7, 6; Demosth., XLVIII, 12; XXXVI, 28; Plato, *Leg.*, IV, 720 C; Lysias, XII, 19; Demosth., XXVII, 9; Schol., Aristoph., *Equt.*, 44.

[40]Hyperides, III, 4 (Oxford); Demosth., XXXVI, 28; Aeschin., I, 97.

[41]Demosth., XXXIV, 5.

[42]Demosth., XXXVI, 28; XLV, 71, 72.

[43][Xen.] *Pol. Ath.*, I, 18.

[44]Demosth., XLV, 71, 72: "You ought to be no less indignant, men of Athens, at the conduct of Phormio, who produced this man as a witness, when you see his impudence and ingratitude. You all know, I take it, that if, when he was for sale, a cook or an artisan in any other trade had happened to purchase him, he would have learned his master's business, and been very far from the prosperity which he now enjoys. But as my father, who was a banker, became his master, and taught him reading and writing, and instructed him in his trade, and put a large property under his management, he has become wealthy" (Kennedy's transl.).

amount *per diem*.[45] Thrifty masters,[46] too, who did not need the services of their own slaves for a short time, sent them over to a friend to earn some extra money, or to the shrine of Eurysaces, whither all the unemployed were wont to gather, free or slave, to wait for a chance employer.[47] In this way "slave labor was kept as mobile as free labor"[48] and the fixed personnel in industry was reduced to a minimum.

Impossible as it would be to calculate the number of slaves in the different trades, there is one fundamental fact about them which makes a general estimate possible—each slave presupposes a master somewhere. The probable number of masters can be approximately determined, and with the aid of the definite instances of individuals mentioned in literature, an average number can perhaps be fixed for the slaves which these masters from the different property classes owned for the purpose of industry.

Care should be taken in an estimate like this of the total number of slaves in Attica by groups, that the numbers in these divisions do not overlap. Those of the middle and the poor classes who lived on a small farm in the country with a slave or two to help indoors and out, and with very little ready money at hand, probably could not afford to own other slaves to be rented to individuals employed in mining or other industry.[49] All their slaves, then, have been reckoned in the preceding chapters. As to the poorest citizens and metics, those who went out by the day to earn their living or practiced a trade of some kind in a small

---

[45][Xen.] *Ath. Pol.*, I, 17; Pollux, VII, 191; Xen., *Mem.*, III, 11, 4; Plato, *Lysis*, 208 A; Diog. Laert., II,531: Χαρμίδου δὲ οἰκέτας αὐτῷ (*sc.* Socrates) διαδόντος ἵνα ἀπ' αὐτῶν προσοδεύοιτο, οὐχ εἵλετο.

[46]Theophrast., *Charact.*, XXX, 7. Plautus, *Asinar.*, 441-43: Dromon mercedem rettulit?—Dimidio minus, opinor.—Quid relicuom?—Aibat reddere, quom extemplo redditum esset; nam retineri, ut quod sit sibi operis locatum efficeret.

[47]Pollux, VII, 133; Philochor., fr. 73 (F. H. G.): τοὺς μισθωτοὺς Κολωναίτας ὠνόμαζον, ἐπειδὴ παρὰ τῷ Κολωνῷ εἱστήκασαν, ὅς ἐστι πλησίον τῆς ἀγορᾶς, ἔνθα τὸ Ἡφαίστειον καὶ τὸ Εὐρυσάκειόν ἐστιν. Bekker, *Anec. Gr.*, II, 212 *s. v.* Ἀνακεῖον: Διοσκούρων ἱερὸν, οὖ νῦν οἱ μισθοφοροῦντες δοῦλοι ἑστᾶσιν.

[48]See·Guiraud, *La Main D'Oeuvre*, etc. (1900), 130.

[49]If any individuals of this lower middle class should have bought slaves on credit for purposes of industry other than for work on their own farms or neighboring ones, and this would be very doubtful, they would, if successful in the venture, be rated soon amongst the next wealthier group or, if unsuccessful, would of course lose the slaves. *V. infra*, 106, note 107.

way at home, I believe that the number of slaves which they could have afforded to own is so small that they may be wholly disregarded in the present calculation.[50] This would restrict the possible masters[51] in this group to the wealthy citizens, to those of the middle class earning a living in the business world, and to all the metics with capital enough to own or to hire slaves, for the metics, debarred from an agricultural life, devoted themselves with great ardor to business.[52]

These considerations show the weakness of any reckoning wherein one takes as a basis the census of 309 B. C., which gives 21,000 citizens and 10,000 metics, and from that reckons in a lump sum three slaves used in industry for each individual citizen and metic, plus a total of 10,000 previously estimated as owned by the same persons and employed in the mines, in addition to 101,000 more owned by the same 31,000 for various other purposes, and regards the total thus reached, that is, 201,000, as a fair estimate of the average number of slaves in Attica throughout the fifth and fourth centuries.[53]

I propose to arrive at an approximate estimate by citing briefly persons actually mentioned in literature as owning a definite number of slave workmen and by investigating their financial condition, to decide for how many others of their wealth and position in society they may perhaps be regarded as typical examples.

For the fifth century there is but one precise datum. Lysias and his brother Polemarchus, two very wealthy metics,[54] in 404

----

[50]See below in this chapter, 103 ff.

[51]The fact that 15,000-20,000 slaves in the fifth century and somewhat less than 10,000 slaves in the fourth century have been already allowed this same group of masters for employment in the mines, should be borne in mind, as well as the fact that slaves constituted only one of the many ways open to capitalists of investing their funds. (*V. infra*, 99, note 62.)

[52]See Glotz, *Le Travail Dans La Grèce Ancienne* (1920), 215 ff., for discussion of the important place which metics occupied in industry.

[53]Wallon, *op. cit.*, 250 ff.; Richter's method is even worse (*op. cit.*, 92 ff.). He reckons, without going into any detailed proof, 100,000 as owned by these 31,000 for industry, besides 50,000 owned by them and employed in the mines, in addition to 100,000 used in household service, another 100,000 owned by the same group for agriculture, and a miscellaneous group of 50,000 owned chiefly by the state as a whole.

[54]Lysias, XII, 19: καὶ ἔχοντες [*sc.* οἱ τριάκοντα] μὲν ἑπτακοσίας ἀσπίδας τῶν ἡμετέρων, ἔχοντες δὲ ἀργύριον καὶ χρυσίον τοσοῦτον, χαλκὸν δὲ καὶ κόσμον καὶ ἔπιπλα

B. C. owned and operated a shield factory employing 120 slaves. This happens to be the largest plant recorded in the literature of the period.

The next in size to this, about which definite numbers are given, is the sword and knife factory owned by the father of Demosthenes (about 360 B. C.), who, as has been stated before, left an estate of more than fifteen talents and was rated, according to his son's own words, among the wealthiest men of his day.⁵⁵ This factory employed thirty-two or thirty-three slaves, bringing in an income of thirty minas (half a talent) a year; besides this, the same man owned a couch factory with twenty slaves, the income from which was twelve minas a year.⁵⁶ This statement throws a little light upon the number of workmen in the shield factory owned by Pasion at about the same time. For besides all his other property, this banker,⁵⁷ one of the richest men in Greece, owned an

καὶ ἱμάτια γυναικεῖα ὅσα οὐδεπώποτε ᾠοντοκτήσασθαι, καὶ ἀνδράποδα εἴκοσι καὶ ἑκατόν, ὧν τὰ μὲν βέλτιστα ἔλαβον, τὰ δὲ λοιπὰ εἰς τὸ δημόσιον ἀπέδοσαν.

These slaves of course represent those who were owned by the family of Cephalus who, with his two sons, lived in Athens thirty years. (Lysias, I, 4). The family was one of the wealthiest of the metics and very prominent in Athenian life (4, 14, 20). They owned three houses (18) having received the honor of ἔγκτησις γῆς καὶ οἰκίας. See also the beginning of Plato's *Respublica* for a description of their home life. At the time that Lysias and his brother were arrested, there were almost four talents in cash in the house, (11) besides the 700 shields in the factory (19). Lysias says the family was proscribed and all of its property confiscated merely because of its great wealth (20).

⁵⁵XXVII, 7: "That the property left me by my father was as much as I have stated, they have themselves given the best proof; inasmuch as they consented on my behalf to be rated at one-fifth of the whole value of my estate, the same percentage at which Timotheus, the son of Conon, and men of the largest fortunes were rated" (Kennedy's transl.).

⁵⁶Demosth., XXVII, 9: ὁ γὰρ πατήρ, ὦ ἄνδρες δικασταί, κατέλιπε δύ' ἐργαστήρια, τέχνης οὐ μικρᾶς, ἑκάτερον, μαχαιροποιοὺς μὲν τριάκοντα καὶ δύ' ἢ τρεῖς . . . ἀφ' ὧν τριάκοντα μνᾶς ἀτελεῖς ἐλάμβανε τοῦ ἐνιαυτοῦ τὴν πρόσοδον, κλινοποιοὺς δ' εἴκοσι τὸν ἀριθμόν, τετταράκοντα μνῶν ὑποκειμένους, οἱ δώδεκα μνᾶς ἀτελεῖς αὐτῷ προσέφερον . . . *Cf. supra*, 52, 53. It should be observed that the twenty couch makers had been pawned to him for a debt of forty minas, that is, he had acquired them incidentally and might not have planned to keep them permanently.

⁵⁷The landed property of Pasion was valued at twenty talents (Demosth., XXXVI, 5); he had thirty-nine talents of his own let at interest (5); his bank yielded an income of 100 minas (11).

ἀσπιδοπηγεῖον, the profit from which was a talent a year.[58] The income from this, which was just twice that from the thirty-three μαχαιροποιοί mentioned above, does not prove conclusively, of course, that the working force was exactly twice as large, but it is not perhaps unreasonable to assume that not many more than sixty slaves were employed in it.

Such was the type of "big business" in Athens. These men, Lysias, Polemarchus, Pasion (metics), and Demosthenes' father, may be taken as examples of the very wealthiest manufacturers of their day, men who operated on the largest scale.[59] Yet the total number of slaves owned for work in their factories by these magnates,[60] for such they seemed to the other Greeks, was about 233 or an average of fifty-eight apiece.[61] But this does not imply that all the members of the wealthiest class, the Pentacosiomedimni, owned an equally large number of slaves employed in some type of industry now under discussion. Many doubtless

---

[58]XXXVI, 11: The words incidentally show that a factory with slaves was considered a safer and more convenient investment than a bank in those days: . . . "The plaintiff acted wisely in choosing the shield-manufactory; for that is a property without risk, whereas the bank is a business yielding a precarious revenue from other people's money" (Kennedy's transl.).

[59]To this same group belong, among others, Ceramon, Nausycides, Cyrebus, Demeas, and Menon mentioned by Xenophon (*Mem.*, II, 7, 6) as having become rich by using purchased barbarians in their factories. No numbers are given.

[60]Demosthenes' own words regarding his father's factories are: τέχνης οὐ μικρᾶς ἑκάτερον (XXVII, 9). Plutarch's description of the man is (*Demosth.*, 4): Δημοσθένης ὁ πατὴρ Δημοσθένους ἦν μὲν τῶν καλῶν καὶ ἀγαθῶν ἀνδρῶν, ὡς ἱστορεῖ Θεόπομπος, ἐπεκαλεῖτο δὲ μαχαιροποιὸς ἐργαστήριον ἔχων μέγα καὶ δούλους τεχνίτας τοὺς τοῦτο πράττοντας. I am tempted to wonder how many pages would have been written about "Demosthenes the Cutler" by investigators of the slave population of Greece and how many hundreds of slaves would have been assigned him for this factory in view of the fact that Plutarch referred to it as ἐργαστήριον μέγα, had we not been fortunate enough to have left us the number of employees stated definitely by his son and heir as thirty-three.

[61]There is no possibility, it will be observed, that these men owned other slaves in industry in addition to these for the numbers have been taken in each instance from a complete inventory of the person's property given in each case by an orator to whose advantage it would have been to represent the amount of property owned as larger even than it actually was. Also it is clear that these slaves belonged not to an individual citizen but to families, *i.e.*, Cephalus and his sons, etc., Demosthenes, Sr., his wife, daughter, and son; Pasion, his wife, son Apollodorus, and freed slave Phormio, so that any estimate of the total should be based upon the number of families in Athens as in Chapter II.

preferred other investments of capital, for example, apartment
houses, farm land, commerce, the mines, or loans at interest.[62]
To estimate the exact proportion of wealthy citizens and metics
who were at any one time engaged in business enterprises which
were comparable to these in the number of slave workmen employed, is of course impossible.

There are several instances, from literature, of persons of enough
property to be classed as rich, who did not own anything as
pretentious as a factory, but yet who had some money invested
in slaves whom they employed in a small way in a shop or
allowed others to hire. Timarchus[63] (about 345 B. C.), whose
property was sufficient to place him with the wealthiest, owned
before he had squandered his riches, nine or ten shoemakers
bringing in two obols a day (the foreman brought in three), one
woman lace-maker who took her wares to market and sold
them, and a man skilled in embroidering. In the estate of Euctemon (about 389 B. C.), totalling about three talents and referred
to in the preceding chapter, there were five or six minas' worth
of slaves[64] for hire, which would mean two or three at the average

---

[62]Aeschines lists these as possible investments open to an honest man (I, 105):
ἀλλ' οὐκ ἔστι τούτῳ λοιπὸν οὐδέν, οὐκ οἰκία, οὐ συνοικία (Cf., Aeschines' definition of
συνοικία I, 124), οὐ χωρίον, οὐκ οἰκέται, οὐ δάνεισμα, οὐκ ἀλλ' οὐδὲν ἀφ' ὧν ἄνθρωποι
μὴ κακοῦργοι ζῶσιν; and Xenophon shows that about the same ones were available
for a woman, since Socrates asks Theodote (Mem., III, 11, 4): ἔστι σοι ἀγρός;
. . . 'ἀλλ' ἄρα οἰκία προσόδους ἔχουσα; . . . ἀλλὰ μὴ χειροτέχναι τινές;
[63]Aeschines (I, 102-4) feels it necessary to explain carefully how Timarchus
happened to be in possession of so much property. He had inherited the possessions of his father and of his uncle Eupolemus (παιδοτρίβης) and had cheated his
blind uncle Arignotus out of everything. Only one of these three estates, it will be
noticed, included any slaves for hire and that one only twelve. The whole list as
given by Aeschines comprised:
     a farm at Sphettus (97), large but run-down,
     a farm at Alopece (97), sold for 20 minas,
     a farm at Cephisia (101),
     a farm at Amphitrope (101),
     two concessions in the mines (101),
     30 minas at interest (100),
     a residence behind the Acropolis (97), sold for 20 minas, besides (97) οἰκέτας
δημιουργοὺς τῆς σκυτοτομικῆς τέχνης ἐννέα ἢ δέκα, ὧν ἕκαστος τούτῳ δύ' ὀβολοὺς
ἀποφορὰν ἔφερε τῆς ἡμέρας, ὁ δ' ἡγεμὼν τοῦ ἐργαστηρίου τριώβολον· ἔτι δὲ πρὸς τούτοις
γυναῖκα ἀμόργινα ἐπισταμένην ἐργάζεσθαι καὶ ἔργα λεπτὰ εἰς τὴν ἀγορὰν ἐκφέρουσαν,
καὶ ἄνδρα ποικιλτήν . . . καὶ ἔπιπλα.
[64]Isaeus, VI, 33. V supra, 80, note 64.

price of slaves.[65] Included in Ciron's possessions (about 363 B. C.), which were valued altogether at more than ninety minas, there were six or seven minas invested in ἀνδράποδα μισθοφοροῦντα (three or four probably).[66] Leocrates (about 330 B. C.), a wealthy man, derived his income mainly from the work of his copper-smiths.[67] These were sold in a hurry for thirty minas, later for thirty-five.[68] They very likely numbered fewer than fifteen.[69]

There are casual allusions to smaller numbers of slaves owned by various people, but we cannot be sure, as we are in the cases previously cited, that they represent the total number owned by these persons for purposes of industry. Therippides, for seven years, one of the three administrators of Demosthenes' estate, claims that he had had three slaves of his own working in the knife factory mentioned.[70] Athenogenes, a wealthy metic from Egypt (about 329 B. C.), owned a slave, Midas,[71] whom he palmed off together with the perfumery shop which the slave with his two sons was managing for him, on an unsuspecting farmer at what seemed a good bargain, but in reality the responsibility of paying five talents of debts incurred by the slave was thus tacitly transferred to the purchaser. Besides these estates which are mentioned as containing slaves, it seems only fair in arriving at a general estimate from a typical group of families that those referred to explicitly as containing none be included in this list.

[65]Xenophon (*Vectigal.*, IV, 23, 24) evidently reckons the average price of slaves to be purchased by the state for unskilled work in the mines according to his plan as 175 drachmas, that is, one and three-fourths minas (Thiel's edition, *Excursus* X). Also see note on p. 47.

[66]Isaeus, VIII, 35. *V. supra*, 53 and 80, note 64.

[67]Lycurgus *c. Leocr.*, 58: οὔτε γὰρ πρότερον οὐδὲ πώποτε ἐγένετο ἐπὶ ταύτης τῆς ἐργασίας, ἀλλ᾽ ἐκέκτητο χαλκοτύπους, οὔτε τότε ἐκπλεύσας οὐδὲν εἰσήγαγεν ἐκ Μεγάρων.

[68]*Id.*, 22, 23, 24. Skilled workmen like these would certainly be worth more individually than mine workers. Demosthenes (XXVII, 9) estimates the makers of knives as worth from three to six drachmas a piece.

[69]With this group there should be mentioned the two shops belonging to Conon. Unfortunately there is no hint given of the numbers. Demosth., XLVIII, 12: "After we had sworn mutual oaths, and the agreement had been deposited with Androclides, I divided the property into two shares, men of the jury. One share consisted of the house in which Conon himself dwelt, and the slaves employed in weaving sackcloth; the other comprised another house, and the slaves employed in grinding colours (φαρμακοτρίβαι)" (Kennedy's transl.).

[70]Demosth., XXVII, 20.

[71]Hyperides, III, 5 (Oxford).

Isaeus furnishes instances of three persons owning mixed estates valued at more than two talents (thus placing the owners among the wealthiest of the country), no one of whom owned slaves who could be classed in this group. Theophon[72] left to his heirs:

a farm at Eleusis, valued at two talents

60 sheep

100 goats

furnishings (ἔπιπλα)

καὶ τὴν ἄλλην κατασκευὴν ἅπασαν.[73]

Stratocles[74] left to his heirs:

a farm at Thriasia, valued at two and a half talents

a house valued at 30 minas

a house at Eleusis, valued at 5 minas

money at interest, 40 minas

sheep, grain, fruits, and so forth,[75] valued at 49 minas.

Theopompus[76] claims that his estate is worth three talents and a half, including two farms, a house, and two talents in money. As has been mentioned before, Aeschines alludes to three estates, only one of which included slaves used in industry. The two estates which he says that Timarchus secured from his uncles Eupolemus and Arignotus seem to have contained no slaves who could be classified in this group.[77]

Here, then, are the estates of twelve representative Athenian families (not individuals), all belonging to the εὔποροι and some even to the πλουσιώτατοι. The slaves that these families owned for the purpose of industry (exclusive of agriculture and the mines) are, with one exception, definitely recorded in literature either as to number or as to money value.[78] The families of Cephalus, Demosthenes, Pasion, Leocrates, Ciron, Euctemon, Timarchus, Stratocles, Theophon, Theopompus, Eupolemus, and

[72]Isaeus, XI, 41.

[73]If slaves are implied in this general word (and that is very doubtful) they have already been included among those who are engaged in agriculture. *V. supra*, 80, note 64.

[74]Isaeus, XI, 42.

[75]*V. supra*, 80, note 64.

[76]Isaeus, XI, 44.

[77]*V. supra*, 99 f.

[78]The exception is Pasion in whose case only the income from his factory is known. *V. supra*, 97, 57.

Arignotus owned together a total of approximately 267 slaves, or about an average of twenty-two for each family.[79] It will be observed that two of these are the wealthiest metics of their times (Cephalus and Pasion), the others are heads of families such as may have lived in Athens at any time, and the nature and variety of their possessions would appear typical. There seems to be no reason why these twelve may not be taken as illustrative of a cross section of the richest class of Athenian residents at any time in the fourth century.

For the middle class, no list of references such as the above can be cited. We can only apply Xenophon's words again, as in the case of slaves in household service:[80] "Those who can afford it buy slaves, that they may have *fellow-workers*." There were no large factories nor mills in Athens employing hundreds of operatives, but only those where employees could be reckoned by the tens. Small shops, separate or a part of the houses of the middle class, formed the real basis of the active industrial life of Athens.[81] In these there worked citizens not devoted to agriculture, and the majority of the metics—people such as those referred to so often by Aristophanes[82] as pale-faced cobblers, tinkers of pots and pans, jewellers, smiths, carpenters, fullers, or tanners. Xenophon[83] refers to their numerical importance in Athenian society when he represents Socrates as urging Charmides not to feel hesitant about addressing the assembly composed as it was of the artisan and

[79]Cephalus..	120	Timarchus	12
Demosthenes	53	Stratocles	0
Pasion	ca. 60	Theophon	0
Leocrates	15	Eupolemus	0
Ciron	4	Arignotus	0
Euctemon	3	Theopompus	0
Total			267

[80]*Mem.*, II, 3, 3: οἰκέτας οἱ δυνάμενοι ὠνοῦνται ἵνα συνεργοὺς ἔχωσι.

[81]See Guiraud (*op. cit.*, especially 90-92), for a study of labor conditions, where he emphasizes the importance of "la petite industrie." Also Glotz, *op. cit.*, 203-13; and Zimmern, *The Greek Commonwealth* (3rd ed., 1922), 257-79.

[82]*Ecclesiaz.*, 248-53; 383-88; *Plutus*, 163-69; 508-26.

[83]*Mem.*, III, 7, 6: "Is it the fullers among them of whom you stand in awe, or the cobblers, or the carpenters, or the coppersmiths, or the merchants, or the farmers, or the hucksters of the market-place exchanging their wares, and bethinking them how they are to buy this thing cheap and to sell the other dear—is it before these you are ashamed, for these are the individual atoms out of which the Public Assembly is composed?" (Dakyns' transl.).

shop-keeping class.[84] These people were in the same position as the farmers: they know exactly how many hands their shops required and to have owned more than were necessary would have been folly.[85] In any case where an unusually large amount of work must be completed in a short time additional persons could easily be hired.[86] From the general evidence in literature it seems reasonable to reckon that, on the average, persons of this class actually owned not more than one slave each for the purpose of assisting in some trade.[87]

The poorest class, and their numbers were large in Athens at all times,[88] was composed of the rest of the independent workmen and the hired laborers. The former were thankful, as Xenophon[89] observes, if they would take on enough work of one kind or another to furnish themselves a living, and for the latter, Iso-

---

[84]See also Xen., *Cyropaedia*, VIII, 2, 5.

[85]*V. supra*, 70.   Xen., *Vectigal.*, IV, 5;

[86]*V. supra*, 95 and notes.

[87]These are the shops where Socrates was so fond of dropping in to chat with the owner (Xen., *Mem.*, III, 10; Plato, *Apolog.*, 22D; Diog. Laert., II, 122): Σίμων 'Αθηναῖος σκυτοτόμος· οὗτος ἐρχομένου Σωκράτους ἐπὶ τὸ ἐργαστήριον καὶ διαλεγομένου τινά, ὧν ἐμνημόνευεν ὑποσημειώσεις ἐποιεῖτο. ὅθεν σκυτικοὺς αὐτοῦ τοὺς διαλόγους καλοῦσιν. Lysias attests the number of these when he says (XXIV, 20) that each of the Athenians is in the habit of spending leisure moments in a favorite shop: ἕκαστος γὰρ ὑμῶν εἴθισται προσφοιτᾶν ὁ μὲν πρὸς μυροπώλιον, ὁ δὲ πρὸς κουρεῖον, ὁ δὲ πρὸς σκυτοτομεῖον, κτλ. Aeschines (I, 24) says that any craftsman moving into a house or shop at once gives a name to the place from the nature of his work: ἐὰν ἰατρὸς εἰσοικίσηται ἰατρεῖον καλεῖται . . . ἐὰν χαλκεὺς χαλκεῖον . . . κναφεὺς κναφεῖον, ἐὰν τέκτων, τεκτονεῖον, κτλ. Whether these men had slaves as assistants or free men does not happen to be mentioned. The emphasis is laid on the fact of a free man, a thinking man, leisurely practicing his trade in a small way, usually in his own house. They hired some free labor, for Lysias (XXIII, 2) incidentally mentions a fuller for whom a man is working who posed as Pancleon, a free man, son of Hipparmodus of Plataea: ἐλθὼν ἐπὶ τὸ γναφεῖον ἐν ᾧ εἰργάζετο προσεκαλεσάμην αὐτὸν πρὸς τὸν πολέμαρχον νομίζων μέτοικον εἶναι. *Cf.* Athen., IV, 168b for other cases where free men are thus employed.

[88]If there be need of ancient testimony on a fact so obvious it is to be found in Plato (*Resp.*, 565A): "The people are a third class, consisting of those who work with their own hands; they are not politicians, and have not much to live upon. This, when assembled, is the largest and most powerful class in a democracy" (Jowett's transl.). See also [Xen.] *Pol. Ath.*, 1.

[89]*Cyropaed.*, VIII, 2, 5: "In a small city the same man must make beds and chairs and ploughs and tables, and often build houses as well; and indeed he will be only too glad if he can find enough employers in all his trades to keep him" (Dakyns' transl.).

crates[90] says, in the good old days the state took a hand in finding them employment in the country or about the city. These were the people of whom the able-bodied ones were ready to go to another city at a moment's notice to help in some emergency construction,[91] who in the fifth century shouted a vote of assent for the expedition to Sicily, as Thucydides[92] remarks, just so they might get a little money for the present and perhaps unlimited wealth in the future, and who, in the fourth century when warfare had to some extent decreased, as discharged soldiers formed a distinct problem for the state.[93] Even a partial list of the poverty-stricken persons mentioned in literature shows the wide variety in types and occupations: the cripple,[94] the widowed wreath-maker,[95] the public crier,[96] the friends of Euxitheus,[97] Cleanthes,[98] blind Arignotus,[99] Eutherus,[100] and the relatives of Euctemon.[101] These and the many others like them may be disregarded in reckoning the masters of the slaves employed in industry.

Upon the basis of this evidence, most of it from the fourth century, I believe that a reasonable even though, necessarily, rather rough estimate can be made for the total number of slaves

[90]VII, 44: "Those who were less well off than others they employed in agriculture and mercantile pursuits, knowing that want of means arises from idleness, and vicious habits from want of means" (Freese's transl.).

[91]Thucyd., IV, 69; V, 82.

[92]Thucyd., VI, 24: . . . "the main body of the troops expected to receive present pay, and to conquer a country which would be an inexhaustible mine of pay for the future" (Jowett's transl.). *Cf.* Aristoph., *Aves*, 592.

They are also the ones who would have been obliged to listen to the taunts of the remnants of the "Ten Thousand" if the suggestion of their leader, Xenophon, was carried out (*Anabas.*, II, 2, 36): "It seems to me that it is only right, in the first instance, to make an effort to return to Hellas and to revisit our hearths and homes, if only to prove to other Hellenes that it is their own fault if they are poor and needy, seeing it is in their power to give to those now living a pauper life at home a free passage hither, and convert them into well-to-do burghers at once" (Dakyns' transl.).

[93]See Zimmern, *The Greek Commonwealth* (3rd ed., 1922), 269, note 1.

[94]Lysias, XXIV.

[95]Aristoph., *Thesmophor.*, 446 ff.

[96]Demosth., XLIV, 3, 4.

[97]Demosth., LVII, 45.

[98]Diog. Laert., VII, 168.

[99]Aeschines, I, 104.

[100]Xen., *Mem.*, II, 8.

[101]Isaeus, V, 39.

in industry in this century, if we reckon twenty-two slaves apiece for all the wealthy families of the citizens and metics, and one apiece for all those of the middle class, again including metics, that is, those of at least hoplite rating.

Now the reforms of Antipater in 322 B. C., as has been observed before, give a definite number for the three upper property classes of citizens. Nine thousand were said to have owned property valued at more than 2,000 drachmas and 12,000 had less.[102] The census of Demetrius in 309 B. C. gives the same total of 21,000 citizens and reports the number of metics as 10,000.[103] Reckoning the same relation between prosperous and non-prosperous metics as for citizens, there would have been possibly 4,000 metics of hoplite rating. As for the two upper property classes of citizens, the Pentacosiomedimni and Hippeis, one can not state positively their numbers at that time, but there is a well-established tradition that there were 1,200,[104] which would leave 7,800 as the numbers for the middle class. The metic population, if divided in the same proportion, would have consisted of about 555 wealthy and 3,445 of the middle class. Dividing these into families as was done in Chapter II[105] when estimating the number of slaves in

---

[102]Diodor., XVIII, 18, 5; Plut., Phoc., 28. V. supra, 60, note 85.

[103]Athen., VI, 272 c.

[104]Harpocration, s. v., χίλιοι διακόσιοι: . . . οἱ πλουσιώτατοι Ἀθηναίων χίλιοι καὶ διακόσιοι ἦσαν οἱ καὶ ἐλειτούργουν. Pollux, VIII, 100.

These were the 1,200 richest citizens who were divided into 20 symmories of 60 men each in 378/7 for the purposes of bearing the state burdens. Demosth., XXI, 155; Harpocration s. v. συμμορίαι. Before that there seems to have been no definite number. There is no exact information of how much property a man must have had to be included in the group; some think from a passage in Demosthenes (XXVII, 1, 64) that for any kind of liturgy two talents were necessary, but Isaeus (V, 31) mentions a trierarch who had but 80 minas and (II, 42) a gymnasiarch with less than 83 minas. Only about 300 (a round number of course) or one-fourth of the group seem to have been of outstanding wealth (perhaps these were the numbers of the Pentacosiomedimni). Demosthenes' reforms, so he says himself, in the matter of the trierarchs, were chiefly concerned with relieving the poorer members of the 1,200 group and making most of the expense fall upon the 300 wealthiest. It was this group of 300 who tried to bribe him not to enforce the new law, as he calls them, "The leaders, the seconds, and the thirds of the symmories." Demosth., XVIII, 102-4; XIV; Aeschin., III, 222; Dinarchus, I, 42. See in general on this subject Brillant's article, "Trierarchia," Daremberg-Saglio Dict., etc. V, 442-65.

[105]See above, 65 ff.

domestic service, there are found to be about 1,040 wealthy families of citizens and metics and 6,759 families of the middle class.[106] Reckoning an average of twenty-two slaves apiece for the former and one slave apiece for the latter, there would be obtained a total of 29,639 or about 30,000 slaves[107] employed in industry during the latter half of the fourth century.

For the fifth century no such definite estimate can be made. According to Meyer's estimate,[108] there would have been 1,650 wealthy families, both citizen and metic, and 22,250 families of the middle class, both citizen and metic. But using Beloch's figures (v. supra, 61, 65), there would have been only 1,050 wealthy families and 10,950 families of the middle class. If the same number of slaves (exclusive of mining) should be allowed each family as was above for the last half of the fourth century, the totals would be 58,550 or 34,050, depending on which estimate of the free population is used. But many of the greatest fortunes[109] of that day were invested largely in the mines, for which 20,000 slaves have been previously reckoned (more than twice as many as at the end of the fourth century), while other business was left largely to the enterprising metics and to a smaller percentage of the citizen body

---

[106] $1,200 \times 3 \div 5 = 720$ families $\Big\}$ of citizens
$7,800 \times 3 \div 5 = 4,680$ families

$533 \times 3 \div 5 = 320$ families $\Big\}$ of metics
$3,465 \times 3 \div 5 = 2,079$ families

[107] I am estimating a total of 30,000 for this group because I do not wish to appear to be minimizing the slave population at Athens, and this seems to represent the maximum permissible. It is hard to see how a number larger than this could reasonably be distributed among the citizens and metics of that day when we consider that with 30,000, provision is made for: 150 wealthy citizens and metics manufacturing on as large a scale as the elder Demosthenes; for all the rest of the citizens and metics of at least one or two talents of property, four slaves apiece (or as many as Ciron owned with his 90 minas plus of property); and for all the remainder of above 2000 drachmas of property (though some clearly lived on farms and were not interested in this type of industry) one slave apiece; with 5,000 slaves left to be distributed among those a little below the 2000 dr. requirement but still able, perhaps, to own a slave. The number 30,000 seems still clearer to be the maximum one permissible when we reflect that for this period 5,000-10,000 slaves have been previously reckoned as owned by the same group and employed in the mines, in addition to 10,000-12,000 owned by them and employed on the farms, to say nothing of those owned for domestic service.

[108] V. supra, 63, 65 ff.

[109] V. supra, 88 ff. Plutarch, Nicias, IV, 2.

than afterwards. The bulk of the population, according to Thucydides,[110] lived in the country and regretfully left their farms to take up their residence in the city. So in spite of the larger population the total number of the masters of slaves of the group now being discussed would have been a much smaller percentage of the whole population than it was a century later. In addition to slaves in the mines, I do not believe that these owners possessed in the fifth century more than 28,000-30,000 slaves (or 18,000-20,000 following Beloch's estimate) for use in all other types of industry, exclusive of agriculture.

During the early part of the Peloponnesian War, the slaves owned for this purpose may have increased in numbers, as citizens began to turn their attention to manufacturing. It is from the literature of this period that complaints first come of wealthy tanners, lamp-makers, and other tradespeople who have become rich over night, acting as demagogues.[111] Even the ravages of the plague[112] and the tremendous expense of the year 428 B. C. for the siege of Potidaea and the maintenance of a fleet of two hundred and fifty ships[113] did not permanently cripple the city financially.[114] Serious economic troubles began only after the expedition to Sicily (415 B. C.) and the occupation of Decelea[115] by the Spartans. Beginning with that time, when the city was cut off from her source of revenue[116] and wealthy citizens had exerted

[110]II, 14; 16.

[111]Aristoph., *Equit.*, 739, 740; "Cleon and Hyperbolus" became almost proverbial for this type of "nouveau riche," *cf. Ran.*, 569, 570; Lucian, *Timon*, 30.

[112]Thucyd., II, 47 ff.

[113]Thucyd., III, 17.

[114]Thucyd., (VI, 26) writes in reference to the expedition to Sicily that in 415 B.C.: "The city had newly recovered from the plague and from the constant pressure of war; a new population had grown up; there had been time for the accumulation of money during the peace; so that there was abundance of everything at command" (Jowett's transl.).

[115]Thucyd., VII, 27; at this time the city was so short of funds that mercenary troops (1300 Thracian targeteers) had to be sent back home even though there was urgent need of using them in an assault on Decelea.

[116]Thucyd., VII, 28: . . . "Through the vast expense thus incurred (*i. e.*, the expedition to Sicily), above all through the mischief done by Decelea, they were now greatly impoverished. It was at this time that they imposed upon their allies, instead of the tribute, a duty of five percent on all things imported and exported by the sea, thinking that this would be more productive. For their expenses became heavier and heavier as the war grew in extent, and at the same time their sources of revenue were dried up" (Jowett's transl.).

themselves to the utmost in fitting out the costly armament that sailed for Sicily,[117] it is certain that the number of slaves was sharply reduced. With mining and agriculture out of the question, there remained only the slaves in household service, and those employed in the city and in service in the fleet.

A passage from Xenophon[118] gives a striking proof of the small number of such slaves in Athens in 406 B. C. News had reached the city of the sad plight of Conon's fleet of forty ships bottled up in the harbor of Mytilene. The people hastily voted (as usual, without taking account of their resources first) to despatch 110 ships to his relief. To fulfill the emergency measure, a conscription lasting thirty days was resorted to, by which every adult male, slave or free, was impressed for service. Now had each ship been manned with its full quota (and that was not always the case)[119] the total number required would have been a little less than 20,000.[120] There is no indication of what percentage of these were slaves but there is one thing certain to be inferred from the passage: there were fewer than 20,000 able-bodied adult male slaves in Athens at that time and almost certainly fewer than even 10,000. After the victory at Arginusae many of these slaves were emancipated and, as some say, admitted as citizens on the same terms as the Plataeans.[121] The troubles after the crushing

---

[117]Thucyd., VI, 31, especially 5: . . . "If anyone had reckoned up the whole expenditure (1) of the state, (2) of individual soldiers and others, including in the first not only what the city had already laid out, but what was entrusted to the generals, and in the second what either at the time or afterwards private persons spent upon their outfit or the trierarchs upon their ships, . . . he would have found that altogether an immense sum amounting to many talents was withdrawn from the city" (Jowett's transl.).

[118]*Hellen.*, I, 6, 24: οἱ δὲ Ἀθηναῖοι τὰ γεγενημένα καὶ τὴν πολιορκίαν ἐπεὶ ἤκουσαν, ἐψηφίσαντο βοηθεῖν ναυσὶν ἑκατὸν καὶ δέκα εἰσβιβάζοντες, τοὺς ἐν τῇ ἡλικίᾳ ὄντας ἅπαντας καὶ δούλους καὶ ἐλευθέρους· καὶ πληρώσαντες τὰς δέκα καὶ ἑκατὸν ἐν τριάκοντα ἡμέραις ἀπῆραν. εἰσέβησαν δὲ καὶ τῶν ἱππέων πολλοί.

[119]Xen., *Hellen.*, I, 5, 20: "When Conon had reached Samos he found the armament in a state of great despondency. Accordingly his first measure was to man seventy ships with their full complement, instead of the former hundred and odd vessels" (Dakyns' transl.).

[120]Meyer, *Forsch. zur Alt. Gesch.*, II, 173. Had there been anywhere near 50,000 slaves at hand at that time it would have been an easy matter to fit out a much larger number of ships than this and besides the word *all* would not have been used when the total number needed for all the crews was less than 20,000.

[121]Aristoph., *Ran.*, 191; Schol. to *Ran.*, 694.

defeat[122] at Aegospotami (405 B.C.) and the influx of needy colonists sent back to Athens by Lysander on purpose to swell the numbers of the starving proletariat,[123] and the ensuing year of political disturbances left little opportunity or wealth to employ slaves in industry. It was not until after 394 B.C. that business conditions in Athens began to improve, as is indicated by the calling in of the bronze coinage.[124]

To sum up briefly, the evidence presented would tend to indicate that in the twenty-five or fifty years preceding the Sicilian disaster, 45,000 to 50,000[124a] represents the maximum number of slaves employed at Athens in gainful occupations, including mining (but exclusive of agriculture); that for the twenty years after the Sicilian disaster, the total number so employed did not exceed 20,000; and that the number gradually increased until in the latter half of the fourth century it reached a maximum of 35,000 to 40,000.

[122]Xen., *Hellen.*, II, 1, 28.

[123]Xen., *Hellen.*, II, 2, 2: "In dealing with the Athenian garrisons, and indeed with all Athenians wheresoever found, Lysander made it a rule to give them safe conduct to Athens, and to Athens only, in the certainty that the larger the number collected within the city and Piraeus, the more quickly the want of necessaries of life would make itself felt" (Dakyns' transl.).

[124]Aristoph., *Ran.*, 725; *Ecclesiaz.*, 819. *V. supra*, 91, note 23; also 93.

[124a]However, if Beloch's estimate of the free population should be used, the total should be placed at 35,000 to 40,000. *V. supra*, p. 106.

CHAPTER V

THE NUMBER OF SLAVES OWNED BY THE STATE

In the interpretation of the few references left us from antiquity which would seem to indicate the numbers of the slaves owned by the state itself there has been much difference of opinion. Wallon (*op. cit.*, 253), for instance, does not include them at all in his total estimate of 201,000 slaves for Athens, while Richter (*op. cit.*, 99) includes them in the 400,000 total as about 50,000. But the consensus seems to be that their number was quite unimportant as compared with the slaves owned by private individuals.

From the ancient lexicographers[1] comes the information that the usual name applied to a state-owned slave was δημόσιος[2] used with or without οἰκέτης,[3] ὑπηρέτης,[4] or some similar word. A certain special group was, for a time, known as Σκύθαι,[5] or τοξόται,[6] and lastly the slave who had the special work of executioner was given the name δημόκοινος,[7] or δήμιος.[8]

There is, apparently, no statement left, telling just when the state, like individual citizens, first bought these slaves to assist in its work, but it is fairly certain that the state did own them in larger or smaller numbers from the sixth century onward. For Herodotus (VI, 121) remarks that a public slave auctioned off the property of Pisistratus to Callias; Antiphon (I, 20) in the fifth century, mentions the executioner, a public slave, Lysias (XII, 19) also alludes to state-owned slaves, and Aristotle, among others, near the close of the fourth century, refers to public slaves (*Pol. Ath.*, 50, 2 and elsewhere).

---

[1]Harpocration, Hesychius, and Suidas *s. v.* τοξόται.

The various duties and names are summarized in Bekker's *Anecdota Graeca* (I, 234), Δημόσιος: ὁ τῆς πόλεως δοῦλος. ἐγίνοντο δὲ Θρᾷκές τινες ἢ Σκύθαι ἢ ἄλλοι βάρβαροι δοῦλοι πρὸς ὑπηρεσίαν τῶν δικαστηρίων καὶ τῶν κοινῶν τόπων καὶ ἔργων. ἐλλειπτικῶς δὲ λέγουσι τὸν δημόσιον, παρέντες τὸν οἰκέτην.

[2]Demosth., XIX, 129.

[3]Aeschin., I, 54.

[4]Aristot., *Pol. Ath.*, 50, 2.

[5]Andoc., III, 5; *v. infra*, 114 f.

[6]Aristoph., *Acharn.*, 54.

[7]Antiphon, I, 20.

[8]Lysias, XIII, 56; Plato, *Resp.*, 439E.

The services[9] rendered the state by these servants seem to have been of three kinds: general clerical work, police duties, and manual labor, so that they may be conveniently discussed under the classification[10] δημόσιοι ὑπηρέται, Σκύθαι, δημόσιοι ἐργάται, although these terms are not quite mutually exclusive.

The first group, whom I shall designate ὑπηρέται, seems to have been used quite generally throughout the fifth and fourth centuries, along with the lowest class of citizens, as clerical assistants to the different magistrates. One office was quite certainly reserved for a slave only, that of executioner or an assistant to οἱ ἕνδεκα. This person, called δημόκοινος or δῆμιος, as has been mentioned, was required to live outside the city limits near the βάραθρον and had the double duty of torturing witnesses and executing criminals.[11] Whether the other assistants of the "Eleven" were slaves or not is a matter of conjecture.[12] Aristotle, however, in his classification of citizens supported by the state under the constitution of Aristides, mentions δεσμωτῶν φύλακες.[13] By this group he appears not to be designating the "Board of Eleven" who had general supervision of the prisons, but a group of citizen assistants used as guards.

Waszynski[14] has shown from the evidence which he has collected

[9]Stephanus Waszynski in a doctoral dissertation entitled *De Servis Atheniensium Publicis* (Berlin, 1898) has discussed thoroughly "quibus et quomodo Athenienses servis publicis usi sunt;" as also has Dr. Oswald Silverio in a Programme entitled *Untersuchungen zur Geschichte der Attischen Staatsklaven* (München, 1900). Neither has attempted to estimate the whole number, though each has assembled considerable data from inscriptions as well as literature.

[10] *Cf.* Waszynski, *op. cit.*, 9.

[11]Antiphon, I, 20; Lysias, XIII, 56; Aeschin., II, 126; Aristoph., *Ecclesiaz.*, 79; Aristot., *Pol. Ath.*, 45, 1; Plato, *Resp.*, IV, 439 E; Plato, *Phaedo*, 116B.

[12]Photius, II, 60 and Bekk., *Anecd. Gr.*, I, 296, *s. v.*παραστάται. These might very properly be discussed with the slaves of the second group, *i. e.*, those performing police duties.

[13]*Pol. Ath.*, 24; *cf.* Plato, *Crito*, 43A where the same expression means watchman: θαυμάζω ὅπως ἠθέλησέ σοι ὁ τοῦ δεσμωτηρίου φύλαξ ὑπακοῦσαι.

[14]On page 15 he has listed concisely the public slaves mentioned or presupposed in the inscriptions, whose duties he has more fully discussed in the pages just preceding. They are:

οἱ δημόσιοι οἱ ἐν ἀκροπόλει   *I. G.*, II, 162 *vs.* 3 *et* 6 *et* 9.

I. G., II, 2 Add. 737 *vs.* 4 *et* 19.

ὁ δημόσιος ὁ ἐν τῷ βουλευτηρίῳ

inferred from Aristot., *Pol. Ath.*, 47, 5; 48, 1;

ὁ δημόσιος ὁ ἐν τῇ Σκιάδι   *I. G.*, II, 476 *vs.* 39;

from the inscriptions that it is safe to assume that the Athenians furnished slaves, if not for every magistrate, at least for the more important ones.[15] The testimony from literature does not contradict this conclusion. Yet the mention always of but one executioner, and the occasional reference to an auctioneer, a secretary in a permanent position, or one assigned to accompany a magistrate on a temporary appointment,[16] or one of the workers in the mint,[17] do not necessarily presuppose any very large staff of slaves assisting each officer of the government. Besides, the freedom evidently accorded those ὑπηρέται might indicate that their numbers were small enough to cause the state no alarm, for their living conditions do not seem to have been much different from those of the lowest class of citizens. Aeschines,[18] in the course of his remarks upon the profligacy of Timarchus, gives a graphic picture of a δημόσιος named Pittalacus. Whatever the nature of the work he was supposed to perform for the state (Aeschines does not mention exactly what it was), it apparently left him time enough to indulge his taste for low amusements and to amass considerable money. He seems to have been allowed to marry and to live in a house of his own as any citizen might. It was possible, too, for such a person's children to become citizens.[19] The scholiast states that the father of Hyperbolus was a public slave, and Lysias[20] mentions as nothing extraordinary the son of a public slave who not only obtained the rights of citizenship but held thereafter an important position in the state.

ὁ δημόσιος ὁ ἐν τῷ μητρῴῳ   I. G., II, 404 vs. 25. 444 vs. 21
    446 vs. 17. 551 vs. 1 et 50; cf. Demosth., XIX, 129.
ὁ δημόσιος ἐν Ἐλευσῖνι   I. G. II, 476 vs. 40.48
ὁ δημόσιος ἐν Πειραιεῖ   I. G., II, 476 vs. 40
ὁ δημόσιος ἐν τοῖς νεωρίοις   I. G., II, 2, 811b vs. 171 et c vs. 135.
Added to these are: ὁ δημόσιος ὁ ἀντιγραφόμενος.

I. G., II, 2, 839; II, 61, 403, 404, 839, 840. Add. 737, 834b, c. IV, 2, 834b. Cf. Demosth., VIII, 47; XXII, 70.

[15]Op. cit., 16: "Cum tot habeamus exempla, concludere possumus Athenienses etsi non omnibus, at tamen maioribus magistratibus servos tales addidisse."
[16]Demosth., VIII, 47; XXII, 70.
[17]Schol., Aristoph., Vesp., 1007.
[18]I, 54 to 61.
[19]Schol., Aristoph., Vesp., 1007.
[20]XXX, 2.

Furthermore, in averaging the number of state-owned slaves employed by officers of the government, it should be borne in mind that slaves did not render all the assistance required. Passages in literature clearly indicate that citizens, probably of the lowest class,[21] were glad to receive the scanty pay with the possibility of promotion afforded by a government position, however humble it might be. Lysias[22] pictures the rise of a shameless ὑπογραμματεύς of servile origin to a position of wealth. This was Nicomachus, appointed for four months to revise and publish the laws of Solon, who managed to extend his term of office to six years and for liberal sums to alter the laws to suit anyone. At the time of the Thirty he fled from Athens, but returned with the restoration of the Democracy to become even more prosperous. The orator Aeschines served at one time in an inferior position as a clerk to a petty magistrate. Demosthenes openly taunts him with this slavish work.[23]

Because the evidence from the inscriptions as collected by Waszynski tends to show that one δημόσιος was assigned to a magistrate, with the exception of the prytaneis and the treasurer of the goddess who had more, and because the references in literature would tend to strengthen that supposition, it is probably safe to agree with Waszynski that the δημόσιοι ὑπηρέται were not much more numerous at Athens than her magistrates.[24] But it is a difficult question to determine how many these magistrates were. There is one definite statement. Aristotle[25] in his classification of

---

[21]Many references to these underlings show that their position was held in contempt: Lys., XXX, 28: Ἁ καὶ ὑμῶν ἔχοι ἄν τις κατηγορῆσαι ὅτι οἱ μὲν πρόγονοι νομοθέτας ἡροῦντο, Σόλωνα καὶ Θεμιστοκλέα καὶ Περικλέα, ἡγούμενοι τοιούτους ἔσεσθαι τοὺς νόμους οἷοί περ' ἂν ὦσιν οἱ τιθέντες ὑμεῖς δὲ Τισαμενὸν τὸν Μηχανίωνος καὶ Νικόμαχον καὶ ἑτέρους ἀνθρώπους ὑπογραμματέας. Antiphon, VI, 35, 48; Demosth., XIX, 70, 200, 237; Aristoph., Ranae, 1084, 1506; Eq., 1103, 1256.

[22]XXX, 27: καίτοι ἀντὶ μὲν δοῦλοι πολίτης γεγένηται, ἀντὶ δὲ πτωχοῦ πλούσιος, ἀντὶ δὲ ὑπογραμματέως νομοθέτης.

[23]XVIII, 209: γραμματοκύφων. 265: ἐγραμμάτευες, ἐγὼ δ' ἠκκλησίαζον; 261: ἐπειδὴ δ' εἰς τοὺς δημότας ἐνεγράφης ὁπωσδήποτε (ἐῶ γὰρ τοῦτο) ἐπειδή γ' ἐνεγράφης εὐθέως τὸ κάλλιστον ἐξελέγω τῶν ἔργων γραμματεύειν καὶ ὑπηρετεῖν τοῖς ἀρχιδίοις.

[24]Op. cit., 22 f. Ex titulis aliisque auctorum locis qui saepissime proferunt, concludere possumus singulis magistratibus singulos servos attributos esse. Nonnullos autem, inter eos et prytanes et quaestores deae plures habuisse ex testimoniis apparet. Itaque numerum omnium publicorum apparitorum haud ita parvum fuisse puto . . . Certius numerum statuere non audeo.

[25]Ath. Pol., 24: ἀρχαὶ δ' ἔνδημοι μὲν εἰς ἑπτακοσίους ἄνδρας.

citizens under the constitution of Aristides, lists 700 officials (ἀρχαί) for the city. It does not seem unreasonable to assume at the outset that this was one of the largest number ever chosen, for Athens was then at the head of an important league and the centre to which legal matters must be brought.[26] Yet 700 seems an incredibly large number, even for that time, when we compare it with the number of officials needed today for a city many times larger than Athens.[27] However, it is probably wise to accept the number from Aristotle as Wilamowitz[28] does, remembering that there were many minor offices in a city like Athens and that perhaps the 700 included besides heads of departments, some of the citizens used as assistants (ὑπηρέται).

If, in addition to the citizen assistants, we assume an average of 700 state-owned slave assistants to these magistrates, I do not believe that we are underestimating their number, understanding of course that at times this number may have varied according to the fortunes of the state even to the extent of several hundred.

The numbers of the group of public slaves called Σκύθαι or τοξόται[29] must next be estimated. This topic has been a subject of much controversy because of the varying interpretations of the definite data left us. Andocides (III, 5), echoed by Aeschines (II, 173), enumerating the many advantages that had accrued to the state since the Persian War, states that "then for the first time we established 300 cavalry and we bought 300 Scythian

---

[26]Cf. [Xen.] Pol. Ath., 3, for the multiplicity of duties attended to by the Athenians.

[27]Athens at this time is supposed to have had a free population not exceeding 100,000 to 150,000. Cf. Beloch., Griech. Geschich., III, I (1922), 274. Now Boston with a total population of 748,000 (official census 1920) uses only 973 on its general administrative staff which includes 24 departments: financial, accounting, inspecting, etc. (letter of Chief Clerk, Statistics Dept., Boston, 1923).

[28]Wilamowitz (Aristoteles und Athen, II, 203, 4) remarks that as for the 700 ἀρχαί, at first sight "die zahl scheint ungeheuer," but after he has listed the various major and minor offices of the state and reckoned the number who might have participated in them he reaches the conclusion: "wie immer er [Aristotle] gerechnet hat, 700 beamte konnte er ganz ohne übertreibung herausbekommen."

[29]These were sometimes called Σπευσίνιοι or Πευσίνιοι. Poll., VIII, 132; Phot. s. v. τοξόται; Schol. to Aristoph., Acharn., 54; Suidas s. v. τοξόται. Bekk., Anec. Gr. s. v. δημόσιοι.

archers."[30] There has been general agreement in accepting these words as indicating that in the fifth century, probably not long after the battle of Salamis, Athens purchased a force of 300 barbarians to serve, as is shown in the numerous references in literature, as a sort of policemen. By means of a rope[31] they are supposed to have helped in gathering the people into the assembly, kept them reasonably quiet when once there,[32] dragged a speaker off the platform when necessary,[33] bound a culprit to a plank[34] when so ordered, and further assisted in keeping the city orderly. But, apparently, they could not lay hands upon a citizen without an order from the officer of the government[35] to whom they happened to be assigned. Aristophanes consistently pictures them as standing about rather helplessly, mentally inactive, and an object of laughter rather than of fear. All this is generally agreed upon; the difference in opinion begins with the rest of the evidence.

For in the same oration, Andocides (and Aeschines again follows him) lists further advantages for the state derived a short time afterwards from the Thirty Years' Peace. This time he states "we established the cavalry at 1200 and τοξότας ἑτέρους τοσούτους."[36] Boeckh[37] and his many followers have interpreted this as meaning that 1,200 cavalry and 1,200 archers were established, Scythian ones just like those mentioned above in (5). Scheibe[38] was apparently the first to object to this interpretation on the grounds that the increase of the Scythians from 300 to 1,200 within twenty years would be too great a financial burden for the state, and that besides, a scholiast to Aristophanes and also Suidas give 1,000[39]

---

[30]Andoc., III, 5: . . . καὶ πρῶτον τότε τριακοσίους ἱππεῖς κατεστησάμεθα καὶ τοξότας τριακοσίους Σκύθας ἐπριάμεθα.

Cf. Aeschin., II, 173: . . . τριακοσίους δ' ἱππέας προσκατεσκευασάμεθα καὶ τριακοσίους Σκύθας ἐπριάμεθα καὶ τὴν δημοκρατίαν βεβαίως εἴχομεν.

[31]Aristoph., Acharn., 22; Ecclesiaz., 378; Pollux, VIII, 104.

[32]Aristoph., Ecclesiaz., 142 f.; Acharn., 54.

[33]Plato, Protagoras, 319 C; Aristoph., Eq., 665; Ecclesiaz., 258.

[34]Aristoph., Thesmophor., 931 ff.; Schol., Thesmophor., 940.

[35]Plato, Protagoras, 319 C.

[36]Andoc., III, 7: χιλίους τε καὶ διακοσίους ἱππέας καὶ τοξότας τοσούτους ἑτέρους κατεστήσαμεν. Cf. Aeschin., II, 174.

[37]Op. cit. (3rd ed.), 264, note a; cf. Schömann, Antiq. Iur. Pub. Gr., II, 224, and Gilbert, Griech. Staatsalt. (2nd ed.), 192.

[38]Philol., III (1848), 542 ff.

[39]Schol., Aristoph., Acharn., 54; Suidas s. v. τοξόται.

and not 1,200 as the number for the Σκύθαι or τοξόται. He suggested that the passage be translated "1200 cavalry and bowmen as many again," *i.e.*, as the 300 Scythians mentioned before, or 600 in all. Thus Scheibe would make the τοξόται of (7) refer to the same kind of τοξόται as in (5). The scholiast's 1,000 might then have arisen, in Scheibe's opinion, from χ¹ the mark indicating 600 being misread as χ(ίλιοι) 1000.[40] Funkhänel[41] soon replied, quoting other passages to show that the expression ἑτέρους τοσούτους refers properly to a number immediately preceding and not to a word so widely separated from it. And so the two troublesome words have been the cause of much uncertainty. Busolt[42] seems to have been the first to object to the number 1,200 for the reason that it is needlessly large for the police of a city like Athens and to maintain on this ground that the τοξόται in the second instance meant the force partly citizen, partly mercenary, which was included in the Athenian army.[43] Waszynski still more plausibly shows that this word τοξόται used with κατεστησάμεθα designates by no means the same group as the Σκύθαι and τοξόται of whom it is definitely said that they were purchased (ἐπριάμεθα).[43] His account, however, of how the 300 originally purchased were increased to 1,000, the number given by the scholiast (Aristoph., *Acharn.*, 54), is rather vague. "Fert annotatio illa Scythas servos publico Athenis mille fuisse. Unde suspicari possumus trecentos illos primos postea in mille suppletos esse. Quo maior urbs ipsa, quo celebrior commeatus Athenarum et Piraei fiebat, eo plures ministri, qui disciplinae publicae consulerent, necessarii erant."

[40]Silverio (*op. cit.*, 37 f.), agrees with Scheibe that 600 is meant, but his explanation that the 1,600 τοξόται (Thucyd., II, 13) included 1,000 citizens and 600 Scythians, which numbers the scholiast confused in copying, is unconvincing.

[41]*Zeitschr. f. Alterthum.*, XIV (1856), 41 ff.

[42]*Griechisch. Staats-und Rechts-Altertum.* (2nd ed., 1892), 310, note 4: "Ein so starkes Skythenkorps wäre nicht ohne Gefahr und auch uberflüssig gewesen."

[43]*Op. cit.*, 30. In a note he gives a short history of the development of this part of the army. Thucyd., II, 3, mentions 1,200 cavalry and 1,600 in the Athenian army at the beginning of the Peloponnesian War. *Cf.* Thucyd., IV, 129, 2; VI, 25, 2; also Plutarch, *Themist.*, 14.

I am inclined to agree with Busolt[44] that 1,000 is much too large a number for the police force of Athens. When we reflect that any citizen had the privilege of coming forward as an accuser of another in all things which affected public interest,[44a] it is evident that no system of secret police was employed or even needed. Their duties, then, consisted wholly in maintaining peace and order in the streets, market, assembly, courts, and public gatherings in general. It appears that they did not even take care of all the policing of the city, for an inscription[45] from about 440 B. C. refers to three citizen τοξόται detailed for sentinel duty at an entrance to the Acropolis to prevent runaway slaves or thieves from entering. Aristotle also mentions fifty citizens used as guards in the city at the time of Aristides.[46] The same author states, too, that the Thirty in organizing their government, in addition to establishing 500 councillors and other officials, including ten magistrates of the Piraeus, chose also a Board of Eleven with 300 assistants to control the prisons, and with these they held the city. The number is significant. These assistants of the Eleven seem clearly to have taken over at this time the duties[47] of the Scythians under

---

[44]I see no reason, however, for agreeing with the rest of his statement (*op. cit.*, 310), that the 200 ἱπποτοξόται mentioned by Thucydides, II, 13 (ἱππέας δὲ ἀπέφαινε διακοσίους καὶ χιλίους ξὺν ἱπποτοξόταις) are the Scythian policemen. Waszynski (*op. cit.*, 32, 33) has assembled strong arguments against such a confusion of terms. The ἱπποτοξόται were distinctly citizens serving with the cavalry and not public slaves.

[44a]See Lofberg, *Sycophancy in Athens* (Chicago-Diss 1917), 1.

[45]*I. G.*, IV, 1, 26a (Dittenberger, *Sylloge* (2nd ed.) 16: . . . φύλακας δὲ [εἶ]ναι τρεῖς μὲν τοξό[τ]ας ἐκ τῆς φυλῆς τῆς [π]ρυτανευούσης. *Cf.* Foucart, "Decret Athénien du Vᵐᵉ· Siècle" *Bull. d. Corr. Hell.* 14 (1890), 177-80 and Gilbert, *op. cit.*, (2nd ed.), 192, note 1.

Wilamowitz (*Aristoteles und Athen*, II, 201) admits "die schützen sind von uns früher mit den gekauften Skythen notwendig verwechselt worden, weil das vierte jahrhundert diese stehende truppe des burgerheeres nicht mehr kennt; aber jetzt sind die inschriftlichen belege nicht mehr vereinzelt." And he even goes so far as to suggest (p. 202, n. 2): "Nun möchte man die schützen, die als huissiers in der volksversammlung auftreten, auch für bürger halten, weil fremde dahin wirklich nicht gehören."

[46]*Ath. Pol.*, 24: καὶ πρὸς τούτοις ἐν τῇ πόλει φρουροὶ πεντήκοντα.

[47]*Ath. Pol.*, 35: τοῦ δεσμωτηρίου φύλακας ἕνδεκα καὶ μαστιγοφόρους τρια[κ]οσίους ὑπηρέτας, κατεῖχον τὴν πόλιν δι᾽ ἑαυτῶν. *Cf.* Xen., *Hellen.*, II, 3, 23, and 54.

the democracy. As in the other instances of 500 councillors, ten magistrates, and the Board of Eleven, one might infer that the customary number of 300 was retained for the police. From comparison with the statistics for police departments of other cities,[48] and the fact that the official duties of this body in Athens were more limited in scope, 300 seems to be an adequate force for the city. It is doubtful if that original number of Scythians specified by Andocides and Aeschines was increased, especially as citizens performed some of the duties usually reserved for policemen.

The words of the scholiast to Aristophanes, *Acharnians,* 54, might at first sight be taken to indicate that 700 more Scythians were later secured. The words are: εἰσὶ δὲ οἱ τοξόται δημόσιοι ὑπηρέται, φύλακες τοῦ ἄστεος, τὸν ἀριθμὸν χίλιοι .... ἐκαλοῦντο οὗτοι καὶ Σκύθαι καὶ Πευσίνιοι ...[49] But another passage from the *Scholia* to the same author, this time to *Lysistrata,* 184, furnishes the useful information: Σκύθας γὰρ καὶ τοξότας ἐκάλουν τοὺς δημοσίους ὑπηρέτας ἀπὸ τῆς ἀρχαίας χρήσεως.[50] From this it is plain that the Athenians used the terms Σκύθαι or τοξόται at first only for the relatively small group for which it was distinctly appropriate, but by a sort of metonymy came finally to apply it to any state-owned slaves. This wider application may have become popular rather quickly

[48]In Boston there are 27 police for every 10,000 inhabitants (Statistics Dept., 1923); Portland, Maine, employs only 20 to every 10,000 (Mayor's office, 1923). Of European cities in 1891, Hirschfeld (*Kl. Schrift.,* 579, note 5) has noted that Paris had 35 policemen for every 10,000 inhabitants, Berlin 32, Brussels 30, London and Vienna each 33 (*Vossische Zeitung,* March 18). Hirschfeld for one, (*op. cit.,* 579) maintains that for ancient Rome the seven cohorts of about 1,000 men each assigned by Augustus, 6 A. D. (Dio, LV, 26) to a *praefectus vigilum,* ostensibly as a fire patrol, actually took over all the duties of policing the city. Hirschfeld then argues that if the city had 1,000,000 inhabitants at that time this would give the high average of 70 policemen to 10,000 persons. The question of the number of Rome's police force is too uncertain, it seems to me, to draw inferences from it as to the conditions in fifth century Athens. (See Mommsen's *Rom. Staats-Recht,* II (3rd ed.), 1055-67.) But the evidence from modern cities would suffice, I should suppose, to make 300 slaves together with such citizens as were specially detailed for such service a more plausible estimate for the police force of Athens than 1000 for a city such as Athens, which is supposed to have had at that time a population (i. e. within the city limits) of from 100,000 to 150,000 (*Cf.* Beloch, *Bevölk.,* 101).

[49]*Cf.* Suidas *s. v.* τοξόται.

[50]Rutherford (*Scholia Aristoph.,* II, 166), I have since noticed, translates to give the same idea: "Observe that the ancient use of Scythians and of bowmen as public attendants led to these names being applied to the public attendants in later times."

from the fact that no descriptive name seems to have been applied to the whole group other than the general term δημόσιοι. So the number 1,000 for the city police could have arisen from the confusion of the two meanings of Σκύθαι, and is valuable in giving an idea of the whole number of slaves owned by the state.

Whatever their number, this group of Scythians was maintained by the state but a comparatively short time, for Aristophanes[51] and Plato[52] seem to be the last to mention them. At any rate, we may be quite sure that at the time of Aeschines and Demosthenes their places were filled by citizens. The former praises the law which requires that at each assembly one tribe sit near the platform to assist in supporting the laws and the democracy, and this φύλη is mentioned elsewhere several times.[53] It is probable that after the resources of the state were seriously impaired by the wars of the last part of the fifth century, this system of police was too expensive to maintain. The state must have had to furnish these barbarians with clothes, food, and lodging,[54] besides buying new slaves each year and the last item might have been a large one after the inroads made by the years of the plague. This might account for the experiment being tried for something less than a century.

There remains to be discussed the last group, the δημόσιοι ἐργάται about which there is little information. The state, unlike its private citizens, seems to have owned no body of slaves to be employed as artisans on its public works, until after the middle of the fourth century. Aside from the fact that none seem to be mentioned in literature, Xenophon[55] implies that there were none at his time. He describes in detail what he terms a new plan for

---

[51]*Ecclesiaz.*, 258, and elsewhere (acted about 393 B. C.).

[52]*Protagoras*, 319 C (probably written before 390 B. C.). Xenophon (*Mem.*, III, 6, 1) refers to the incident of Glaucon being dragged off the platform but whether by τοξόται or not he does not state. Wilamowitz suggests, as I have mentioned, (*supra*, 117, note 45) that perhaps these τοξόται after all were citizens, as foreigners would not belong in an assembly.

[53]Aeschin., I, 33; III, 4; Demosth., XXV, 90. There is no mention of any body of assistants, slave or free, which this tribe may have had at hand to assist in removing objectionable speakers from the platform.

[54]*V. supra*, 47.

[55]*Vectigal.*, IV, 17 f: τοῦτο ἂν μόνον καινὸν γένοιτο εἰ ὥσπερ οἱ ἰδιῶται κτησάμενοι ἀνδράποδα πρόσοδον εἶναι ἀέναον κατασκευασμένοι εἰσίν, οὕτω καὶ ἡ πόλις κτῷτο δημόσια ἀνδράποδα.

increasing revenues. The state is advised to buy slaves and let them out at a definite price to workers of the mines at Laurion. Seeking a comparison to support his scheme, he says that the state, just as individuals now do, should invest in slaves. If there had been any state-owned workmen then, it seems as though he would not have insisted that the only new part to the scheme was that the state, not the individual, was to invest in slaves.[56]

Inscriptions[57] beginning with 329/8 B.C. and 317 B.C. show public workmen employed in repairing temples. Aristotle[58] speaks of δημόσιοι ἐργάται assigned to the road commissioners but he gives no clue as to how many these officials needed. The first of the inscriptions referred to, shows seventeen slave workmen, the second, twenty-eight. We might perhaps infer from this that the numbers of these artisans increased at the end of the fourth century, but any more definite estimate must for the present be guess-work.

At any rate, we may venture to conclude that the numbers of state-owned slaves were about the same during the fifth and fourth centuries. After the discontinuance of the Scythian police force, which numbered about three hundred, at some time during the fourth century, there seem to have been employed in the public works of various kinds, slave workmen,[59] who, taken with the other δημόσιοι (estimated at about seven hundred) appointed as under-

---

[56]The Schol. on Aristoph., *Vesp.*, 1007, mentions the father of Hyperbolus as slaving in the mint, but there is no reason to infer that he was not doing the type of work included in the discussion of ὑπηρέται: . . . οὗ ὁ μὲν πατὴρ ἐστιγμένος ἔτι καὶ νῦν ἐν τῷ ἀργυροκοπείῳ δουλεύει τῷ δημοσίῳ.

[57]*I. G.*, II, 2 Add. 834b (329/8 B. c.); IV, 2, 834b; II, 2 Add. 834c (317-307 B. c.).

[58]*Ath. Pol.*, 54 (written probably between 329-25): κληροῦσι δὲ καὶ τάσδε τὰς ἀρχάς. ὁδοποιοὺς πέντε οἷς προστέτακται δημοσίους ἐργάτας ἔχουσι τὰς ὁδοὺς ἐπισκευάζειν.

[59]Aristotle remarks that as at Epidamnus, so at Athens, a system was once introduced of state-owned workmen for the public works. *Polit.*, II, 4, 13: ἀλλ' εἴπερ δεῖ δημοσίους εἶναι, τοὺς τὰ κοινὰ ἐργαζομένους δεῖ (καθάπερ ἐν 'Επιδάμνῳ τε, καὶ Διόφαντός ποτε κατεσκεύαζεν 'Αθήνησιν) τοῦτον ἔχειν τὸν τρόπον. Waszynski (*op. cit.*, 41) argues plausibly that this was the Diophantus mentioned by Demosthenes, XIX, 403, 436; XX, 498, and living from 370-30 B. c. But until the Diophantus mentioned is more definitely identified we can not be certain when this experiment was first tried.

lings to the magistrates, probably totalled about 1,000. This is the most reasonable explanation of the statements of the Scholiast on Aristoph., *Acharn.*, 54 and *Lysistr.*, 184, and there appears to be nothing in the inscriptions or in general literature which requires us to assume that the number of slaves owned by the state was any larger.

CHAPTER VI

THE NUMBER OF SLAVE CHILDREN

In any estimate of the whole slave population according to their occupations there should be taken into consideration the number of children, that is, of those who were too young to be of profitable assistance to their masters, in which class there would be included all slaves under nine or ten years of age. Their numbers would not be as large as might be expected from comparison with other slave systems, as it is a well-recognized fact that Athens, using her slaves as she did chiefly for industrial purposes, did not consider it economy to rear them, but rather recruited them from capture in war or by piracy, by enslaving metics or citizens who failed to meet certain legal obligations or, as was most commonly the case, by direct purchase of barbarians.[1] From the nature of the evidence available it is impossible to give other than a very general notion of the size of this group.

Slaves born in the house were called οἰκότριβες[2] or οἰκογενεῖς[3] and their number depended, of course, upon how many women slaves were in the master's possession and his leniency toward them.[4] In domestic service women slaves probably formed a majority,[5] but in agriculture[6] as well as other phases of industry[7]

---

[1]For a discussion of the evidence for this see Thalheim, *Pauly-Wissowa R. E.* V, col. 1789, *s. v.* δοῦλοι; Busolt, *Gr. Staatskunde*, 275; and especially Becker-Göll, *Charicles* (1878), III, 10-13; Schömann-Lipsius, *Griechische Alterthümer* (1897), I, 366 f.

[2]Suidas, *s. v.* οἰκότριψ, Bekker, *Anecd. Gr.*, I, 286, 18: οἰκότριβες οἱ οἰκέται καλοῦνται οἱ δοῦλοι ἐκ δούλων γενόμενοι, οἱ οἰκογενεῖς.

[3]Plato, *Menon*, 82B; Socrates asks Menon concerning a slave: Ἕλλην μέν ἐστι καὶ ἑλληνίζει; and Menon answers: πάνυ γε σφόδρα, οἰκογενής γε.

[4]A wife was regarded as a proper possession of a free man only ([Aristot.] *Oec.*, 2). The plaintiff in a case of assault and battery against Evergus and Mnesibulus tries to prove that the aged nurse is no longer a slave but free by saying (Demosth., XLVII, 72): οὐδ' ἂν θεράπαινά γε· ἀφεῖτο γὰρ ὑπὸ τοῦ πατρὸς τοῦ ἐμοῦ ἐλευθέρα καὶ χωρὶς ᾤκει καὶ ἄνδρα ἔσχεν.

[5]*V. supra*, Chapter II.

[6]Demosth., LVII, 45. *V. supra*, Chapter III.

[7]Aeschin., I, 97. One woman lace-maker is mentioned but it should be observed also that even in this industry where women might be expected to predominate, the only other employee known is a man, skilled in embroidering, who belonged to the same estate. *V. supra*, Chapter IV. *Cf. infra*, 124, note 16.

they were employed in limited numbers, while in connection with
the mining industry,[8] because of the severity of the conditions of
employment, I presume that their numbers may be regarded as
almost negligible.[9]

As for the attitude of the masters, it can be stated with some
assurance that the Athenians considered it more profitable to buy
slaves than to rear them, and prudent masters, therefore, attempted to keep the privilege of a so-called wife and of children
as a reward in store for faithful slaves.[10] However, due to the
extraordinary freedom which slaves at Athens enjoyed,[11] the
number of slave children was probably not as limited as the
masters could have desired, and laws had to be passed to settle the
technical questions as to which master owned a child born of two
slaves belonging to different individuals, or the status of a child,
one of whose parents was a slave and the other a free person.[12] As
a matter of fact, in some households, principally in the country,
where there were both men and women slaves in domestic service
and agriculture, where the cost of rearing a child was less than
in the city, and the master was especially lenient, there may have
been a considerable number of slave children.[13]

Two incidents alluded to by the orators would imply that it was
impossible to distinguish slave children from free by dress, speech
or appearance and that they were numerous enough to cause
persons to mistake one for the other. For in the oration against
Nicostratus, Apollodorus, son of Pasion, alleges against the defend-

----

[8]See first half of Chapter IV (*supra*).

[9]See Beloch. *op. cit.*, 54, Hume, *op. cit.*, 391 ff.

[10]Xen., *Oec.*, XX, 5: "Then I showed her the women's apartments, separated
from the men's apartments by a bolted door, whereby nothing from within could
be conveyed without, clandestinely, nor children born and bred by our domestics
without our knowledge and consent—no unimportant matter, since, if the act of
rearing children tends to make good servants still more loyally disposed, cohabit-
ing but sharpens ingenuity for mischief in the bad" (Dakyns' transl.).

[Aristot.] *Oec.*, I, 5: "And just as all other men become worse when they get
no advantage by being better, and there are no rewards for virtue and punish-
ments for vice, so it is with slaves. . . . One ought to bind slaves to one's
service by the pledges of wife and children" (Forster's transl.).

[11]Aristoph., *Ecclesias.*, 721; [Xen.] *Ath. Pol.*, I, 10; Plautus, *Stichus*, 446 ff.

[12]Plato, *Leg.*, XI, 930.

[13]In the will of Aristotle, for example, there are three children mentioned
(Diog. Laert., V, I, 9).

ant and his brother: "In addition to this, as they were neighbors, and my farm was adjacent to theirs, they sent into it in the day-time, a young boy, the son of a citizen, and desired him to pluck off the flowers of my rosary, so that, if I caught him, and struck him in a passion, or put him in bonds, taking him for a slave, they might bring an indictment for outrage against me."[14] In the other case the injured party claims: "And they not only went off with my furniture, men of the jury; they were taking away my son also, as if he had been a slave, until Hermogenes, one of my neighbors, met them and told them that he was my son."[15]

But taking the slave population as a whole and considering its relatively small proportion of women, coupled with the fact that the majority of the slaves were employed in industry for which it would not have been profitable to breed slave labor,[16] the recourse available of exposure of infants, and the probable higher rate of infant mortality at that time, it is likely that the percentage of slave children under eight or nine years of age was hardly equal to that of a country today, where the population of all freemen is steadily increasing and the numbers of men and women are about equal.[17] In the case of our own population which would, in one way, offer a parallel to the slave population of Athens, because due to immigration, the percentage of adults in the total population is abnormally high,[18] it has been calculated that approximately twenty-two percent of the total population is under nine years of age.[19] But it is an admitted fact that women in an aver-

[14]Demosth., LIII, 16 (Kennedy's transl.).

[15]Demosth., XLVII, 61 (Kennedy's transl.).

[16]That is, children are useful on a farm in many ways at an age much earlier than that in which they may be profitably employed in industry. In fact we have no evidence that children were employed at all in Athenian factories, although it is possible that a few worked at light tasks. Had, however, the number of slave children been as large as those of an ordinary free community, they must have been so employed, and it is hardly possible that no mention whatever would have been made of them.

[17]Aristotle mentions that the numbers of men and women were equal in his day, and in the statement clearly implies, as Beloch suggests (op. cit., 54), that the same was not the case with the slave population. His words are (Polit., I, 5, 12): αἱ μὲν γὰρ γυναῖκες ἥμισυ μέρος τῶν ἐλευθέρων.

[18]For a discussion of this, see 14th Census of the United States (1920), Vol. II, 146.

[19]14th Census of the United States (1920), Vol. II, 16: 1900, 23.8%; 1910, 22%; 1920, 21.7%.

age growing population such as ours constitute one-half of the whole number.[20] So in the case of the slave population at Athens, where women were probably fewer than one-fifth of the whole number,[21] as Wallon[22] (*op. cit.*, p. 251) has estimated them, the percentage of children should be correspondingly reduced. At the normal rate[23] then of a country like the United States, there would have been for the possible 16,200-18,200 slave women of the total 71,000-91,000 adult slaves[24] estimated for Athens in the fifth century from 9,720-10,920 children under nine or too young to be employed usefully; for the 10,800-12,600 women of the 54,000-63,000 adult slaves reckoned for the last half of the fourth century, there might have been 5,350 to 7,230 children. Or as we are dealing here with approximate numbers: 9,000-10,000 slave children (under nine) in the age of Pericles;[24a] 6,000 to 7,000 in the age of Alexander.

[20]Census, 1920 (*l. c.*).

[21]Cephisodorus, a metic living in the Piraeus in 415 B. C. owned, as it appears from the auctioneer's list (*v. supra*, 80), sixteen slaves, probably for industrial purposes of some sort. Of these there were ten or eleven men (the reading is uncertain) three or four women, and two children, a distribution of sexes and ages, which, I suppose, may be regarded as typical in such a group.

[22]*Cf.* Beloch, *Bevölk.*, 54.

[23]That is, reckoning that among every one hundred persons in the United States there are: 22 under nine, 39 women and 39 men over nine, but that in Athens out of 100 slaves there were, owing to the fact that the men exceeded the number of women five times: 9 – children, 15 + women, 76 – men. This reckoning clearly will give maximum numbers, as, for the reasons cited above, it would be very doubtful if the number of births among slaves equalled that of a free population.

[24]*V. infra*, 126 f.

[24a]Using the 59,700-70,000 total of adult slaves (*v. infra*, 126) based on Beloch's estimate (*v. supra*, 61, 65) of the population, there would have been, by the same reckoning 7,164-8,400 slaves under nine years of age, or in round numbers 7,200-8,500.

CONCLUSION

The general evidence from the literature of the period, presented in the preceding chapters, confirms the supposition that the number of slaves employed at Athens, a term which is here used as synonymous with Attica, varied considerably at different periods during the fifth and fourth centuries before Christ, and stood in direct relation to the size of the free population and the general economic conditions. The evidence further supports two conclusions; first, that slaves were purchased, primarily, as one of the many ways available of investing capital profitably, and not for the purposes of ostentation and luxury; and secondly, that a large percentage of the free population, from lack of funds, were obliged themselves to work at all kinds of occupations, to secure the necessities of life.

In the fifth century, after the Persian Wars, and before the disasters of the Peloponnesian War, when the mines were in their most prosperous condition (Xen., *Vectigal.*, IV, 25) and agriculture was as flourishing as was possible (Thucyd., II, 15) in a land so unproductive naturally as Attica (Aeschyl., *Pers.*, 790-92), and furthermore when Athens, at the head of an important league, was the principal centre of commerce for the Aegean World ([Xen.] *Ath. Pol.*, II, 11, 12) the slave population reached its greatest expansion. This population has been estimated by groups, according to occupation, that is, whether working for the state in any capacity, or for a private individual in household service, in agriculture, or in any other form of industry (including mining), and the following totals, varying in two instances only, because on the numbers of the slave-owning population of the fifth century scholars (*v. supra*, 60 ff. and notes) are not yet agreed, have been reached as approximate maximum estimates:

	Reckoned from Meyer's estimate of free population (*v. supra* 61 ff.)	Reckoned from Beloch's estimate of free population (*v. supra* 61 ff.)
Slaves owned by the state	700— 1,000	700— 1,000
Slaves employed in household service	29,000— 30,000	16,000—17,000
Slaves employed in agriculture	10,000— 12,000	10,000—12,000
Slaves employed in mining	15,000— 20,000	15,000—20,000
Slaves employed in other industry	28,000— 30,000	18,000—20,000
Children under nine years of age	9,000— 10,000	7,200— 8,500
	91,700—103,000	66,900—78,500
	or in round numbers 97,000	or in round numbers 73,000

This would mean that the number of slaves in the age of Pericles was one-half that of the total free population of Attica (*v. supra*, 63 f.). In other words, each of the 23,900 families, citizen and metic, reckoned from Meyer's high estimate (*v. supra*, 63) of those with property enough to be rated as Zeugites (*v. supra*, 48 and 57) could have owned, on the average, four slaves apiece, with a few thousand slaves left to be distributed among families who lacked only a little of being classed with the Zeugites. Using Beloch's more conservative estimate, however, (*v. supra*, 65, note 99) of 20,000 persons, citizens and metic, of Zeugite rating, each of these 12,000 families (*v. supra*, 63) could have owned an average of six slaves apiece, with a few thousand left to be divided among the Thetes as above (*v. supra*, 57).

For the period roughly designated as 415 B. C. to 394 B. C.—from the Sicilian disaster to Conon's victory and the calling in of the bronze coinage—the slave population, due to the extraordinary temporary decrease in population and wealth, has been estimated in a general way as about one-third as large as the totals given for the preceding period.

With the reorganization of business, the increase in the output of the silver mines (Xen., *Vectigal.*, IV, 28) which, however, chiefly due to lack of capital (Xen., *Vectigal.*, IV, 28; V, 12), never equalled that of the fifth century, and the general prosperity which began just before the middle of the fourth century and continued throughout the administration of Lycurgus, the number of slaves has been shown to have increased from the lowest levels reached at the beginning of the fourth century, but, as in the case of the citizen population, not to have attained the height of the age of Pericles.

There have been reckoned for this time:

Slaves owned by the state	700- 1,000
Slaves employed in household service	12,000-14,000
Slaves employed in agriculture	8,000-10,000
Slaves employed in mining	5,000-10,000
Slaves employed in other industry	29,000-30,000
Children under nine years of age	6,000- 7,000
Totals	60,700-72,000
	or in round numbers
	60,000-70,000

In the latter half of the fourth century, then, the total number of slaves was considerably more than half that of the free population as usually reckoned (*v. supra*, 60). Each of the 7,800 families (*v. supra*, 106, note 106), citizen and metic, who possessed 2,000 drachmas in 322 B. C., in other words, an income of 240 drachmas, when about 360 drachmas were necessary yearly for a working-man's family (*v. supra*, 34, note 128) could have owned, on an average, eight slaves, with a few thousand slaves left to be distributed among the Thetes (*v. supra*, 57).

The scanty, direct statistical evidence from these two centuries, far from refuting these general estimates, strongly supports them. With a number for the slave population of the fifth century such as has been indicated, the words of Thucydides (VIII, 40) that wealthy Chios had a larger slave population than any country except Lacedaemon become reasonable; the same historian's statement that the flight in 413 B. C. of 20,000 slaves, most of them artisans (VII, 27, 18) caused great economic distress in Athens is easily understood; and the extraordinary liberty accorded to slaves at Athens ([Xen.] *Ath. Pol.*, I, 10) in direct contrast to their harsh treatment at Chios, where offences had to be "more severely punished because of their number" (Thucyd., VIII, 40) becomes explicable. The census of 378/7 B. C. taken in Attica during a period of economic decline (Polyb., II, 62 and corroborated by Demosthenes [in 354 B. C.] XIV, 19), which gives approximately 6,000 talents as the value of the land, houses, and all the rest of the property in the hands of private individuals, becomes possible with the number of slaves at 50,000 or less at that period. With the average annual importation of about 800,000 medimni of grain as stated by Demosthenes (XX, 31) and the wheat and barley raised on the tillable fourth part of Attica's surface, which for at least one year, 329/8 B.C. (*I.G.*, IV,[2] 834b, II), amounted to approximately 400,000 medimni, food enough could be provided for a population in Attica estimated in the latter part of the fourth century as consisting of about 93,000 free inhabitants and 60,000 to 70,000 slaves. Finally, with these estimates it is possible at any time in the two centuries for a wealthy man to have owned, as Plato says (*Resp.*, IX, 578E), "more than fifty slaves" and yet for a poor man to have had, as Aristophanes says (*Ecclesiaz.*, 593), "not even one."

SELECTED BIBLIOGRAPHY[1]

For this thesis all of the Greek authors of the fifth and fourth centuries before Christ have been excerpted[2], as well as the chief subsidiary historical and philosophical writers of later centuries whose works would be likely to contribute any statement of importance to this subject.

É. Ardaillon, *Les Mines du Laurion dans l'Antiquité.* Paris, 1897.

L. Beauchet, *Histoire du Droit Privé de la République Athènienne.* Paris, 1897. 4 vols.

W. Becker, *Charikles.* Neubearbeitet von Hermann Göll. Berlin, 1878. 3 vols.

J. Beloch, *Die Bevölkerung der Griechisch-Römischen Welt.* Leipzig, 1886.

—————, "Das Volksvermögen von Attika," *Hermes,* XX (1884), 237-61.

—————, "Griechische Aufgebote," *Klio,* V (1905-6), 341-74.

—————, *Griechische Geschichte* 2. neugestalt. Aufl., I-III. Berlin and Leipzig, 1913-23.

G. Billeter, *Geschichte des Zinsfusses im Griechisch-Römischen Altertum bis auf Justinian.* Leipzig, 1898.

F. Blass, *Die Attische Beredsamkeit.* 2. Aufl. Leipzig, 1887-98. 3 vols.

A. Böckh, *Die Staatshaushaltung der Athener.* 3 Aufl. von Max Fränkel. Berlin, 1886. 2 vols.

H. Bolkestein, *Fabrieken en Fabrikanten in Griekenland.* Groningen, 1923.

G. Busolt, *Griechische Staatskunde.* 3. Aufl., Erster Hauptteil, Handbuch der Klassischen Altertums-Wissenschaft. IV, 1, 1. hrsg. von Ivan von Müller. München, 1920.

—————, *Griechische Geschichte.* 2. vermehrte und völlig umgearbeitete. Aufl., Gotha, 1895. 3 vols.

B. Büchsenschütz, *Besitz und Erwerb im Griechischen Alterthume.* Halle, 1869.

A. Calderini, *La Manomissione e la Condizione dei Liberti in Grecia.* Milan, 1908.

M. Cavaignac, *Études sur l'Histoire Financière d'Athènes au Ve. Siècle.* Paris, 1908.

E. Ciccotti, *Il Tramonto della Schiavitù nel Mondo Antico.* Torino, 1899. French Transl. by G. Platon. Paris, 1910.

—————, "Del Numero degli Schiavi nell'Attica." *Rendiconti dell'Istituto Lombardo,* Ser. II, XXX (1897), 555-573.

M. Clerc, *Les Métèques Athéniens.* Paris, 1893.

H. Clinton, *Fasti Hellenici.* II, 468-526, 3rd ed. Oxford, 1841. 3 vols.

W. Ferguson, *Greek Imperialism.* Boston and New York, 1913.

—————, *Hellenistic Athens, An Historical Essay.* London, 1911.

H. Francotte, *L'Industrie dans la Grèce Ancienne.* Bruxelles, 1900.

P. Foucart, "Note sur les Comptes d'Eleusis." *Bulletin de Correspondance Hellenique,* VIII (1884), 194-216.

---

[1]These are the works which have been of the greatest assistance in preparing this thesis. The others to which occasional reference has been made, will be found cited in the notes wherever any quotation is given.

[2]A few of the scientific writings of Aristotle and Theophrastus have been omitted which from their subject matter would not be likely to contain any statement of importance to this investigation.

L. GERNET, "L'Approvisionnement d'Athènes en Blé au Ve et au IVe Siècles." *Mélanges d'Histoire Ancienne*, XXV, 273-326. Paris, 1909.

G. GILBERT, *Griechische Staatsalterthümer*. 2. Aufl., Leipzig, 1893. 2 Vols. Eng. transl. by E. Brooks and T. Nicklin. London, 1895.

G. Glotz, *Le Travail dans la Grèce Ancienne*. Paris, 1920.

——————, *La Solidarité de la Famille en Grèce*. Paris, 1904.

W. GREENE, *The Achievement of Greece*. Cambridge, 1923.

P. GUIRAUD, *La Main-d'Oeuvre Industrielle dans l'Ancienne Grèce*. Paris, 1900.

——————, *Études Économiques sur l'Antiquité*. Paris, 1905.

——————, *La Propriété Foncière en Grèce jusqu'à la Conquête Romaine*. Paris, 1893.

W. HEITLAND, *Agricola*. Cambridge, 1921.

P. HERFST, *Le Travail de la Femme dans la Grèce Ancienne*. Diss. Utrecht, 1922.

D. HUME, "Of the Populousness of Ancient Nations." London, 1752. Essays Moral, Political, and Literary by David Hume. Edited by T. H. Green and T. H. Grose. I, 381-443. London, 1898.

F. JEVONS, "Work and Wages in Athens." *Journal of Hellenic Studies*. XV (1895), 239-47.

J. LETRONNE, "Mémoire sur la Population de l'Attique pendant l'Intervalle de Temps compris entre le Commencement de la Guerre du Peloponnese et la Bataille de Chéronée." *Mém. de l'Acad. d. Inscrip. et Belles-Lettres*, VI (1822), 165-220.

J. LIPSIUS, "Die Attische Steuerverfassung und das Attische Volksvermögen." *Rheinisches Museum für Philologie*, LXXI (1916), 161-86.

A. MAURI, *I Cittadini lavatori dell'Attica nei Secoli 5° e 4° A. C.* Milan, 1895.

E. MEYER, *Die Sklaverei im Altertum*. Dresden, 1898. Republished in *Kleine Schriften zur Geschichts-theorie*, 169-212. Halle, 1910.

——————"Die Bevölkerung des Altertums." Handwörterbuch der Staatswissenschaften, herausgegeben von Conrad, etc. II, 443-456. Jena, 1890-94.

——————, "Die Wirtschaftliche Entwicklung des Altertums," *Kleine Schr. u. s. w.* Halle, 1910.

——————, "Wehrkraft, Bevölkerungszahl und Bodencultur Attikas." *Forschungen zur Alten Geschichte*, II, 148-95. Halle, 1899.

——————, *Geschichte des Altertums*. Stuttgart and Berlin, 1897-1909. 5 vols.

O. NEURATH, *Antike Wirtschaftgeschichte*. 2. Umgearb. Aufl., Leipzig, 1918.

W. A. OLDFATHER, "Social Conditions and Theories in the Graeco-Roman World," III. "Slavery as an Economic Institution." *The Progressive Journal of Education*, II (Dec. 1909-Feb. 1910), 116-25.

W. PATERSON, *Nemesis of Nations*. London, 1907.

W. RICHTER, *Die Sklaverei im Griechischen Altertume*. Breslau, 1886.

J. SACO, *Historia de la esclavitud desde los tiempos más remotos hasta nuestros días*. Paris, 1875-77. 3 vols.

G. SCHÖMANN, *Griechische Alterthümer*. 4. Aufl. neubearb. von J. Lipsius. Berlin, 1897-1902.

A. SCHAEFER, *Demosthenes und seine Zeit*. 2. revidierte Ausg. Leipzig, 1885-87. 3 vols.

O. SILVERIO, *Untersuchungen zur Geschichte der Attischen Staatsklaven*. Gymn. Progr. Munchen, 1900.

L. VAN HOOK, "Was Athens in the Age of Pericles Aristocratic?" *Classical Journal*, XIV (1919), 472-97.

—————, *Greek Life and Thought*. New York, 1923.

H. WALLON, *Histoire de l'Esclavage dans l'Antiquité*. 2nd ed. Paris, 1879. 3 vols.

S. WASZYNSKI, *De Servis Atheniensium Publicis*. Inaug. Diss. Berlin, 1898.

—————, "Uber die Rechtliche Stellung der Staatsklaven in Athen." *Hermes*, XXXIV (1899), 553-67.

U. VON WILAMOWITZ-MÜLLENDORFF, *Aristoteles und Athen*. Berlin, 1893. 2 Vols.

S. ZABOROWSKI, "Ancient Greece and its Slave Population." *Revue Anthropologique* XXI (1911), Transl. in *Annual Report* . . . *Smithsonian Institute*, etc. (1912), 597-608.

A. ZIMMERN, "Was Greek Civilization Based on Slave Labour?" *Sociological Review*, II (1909), 1-19, 159-76.

—————, *The Greek Commonwealth*. 3rd ed. Oxford, 1922.

VITA

Rachel Louisa Sargent was born February 10, 1891, at Methuen, Massachusetts, where she received both her grammar school and high school education. In 1907-8, as a post-graduate student in languages, she attended Robinson Seminary, Exeter, New Hampshire, and in 1909 entered Bates College from which she was graduated in 1914 with final honors in Language and Literature. Before and during her college course, she taught approximately three years in the schools of Maine and New Hampshire. In her senior year, she served as an assistant in Latin at Bates College, and for two years after graduation was an instructor in Westbrook Seminary, Portland, Maine. At the University of Illinois, in 1916-17, she was a Scholar in Classics, taking the master's degree in 1917. From 1917 to 1920 she was an instructor in Latin at Champaign High School, Illinois, and from 1920 to 1922 held a similar position at Shortridge High School, Indianapolis. Since that date, she has been in residence at the University of Illinois as a graduate student and instructor in Spanish and Latin at the University High School. Her work at Illinois has been done under the direction of Professors H. J. Barton, H. V. Canter, J. D. Fitz-Gerald, C. M. Moss, W. A. Oldfather, and A. S. Pease.

INDEX